# THE APOSTOLIC
# MINISTRY

## by

# RICK JOYNER

# THE APOSTOLIC MINISTRY

# RICK JOYNER

**MorningStar Publications**
A DIVISION OF MORNINGSTAR FELLOWSHIP CHURCH
P.O. Box 440
Wilkesboro, NC 28697

*The Apostolic Ministry*
Copyright © 2004 by Rick Joyner
Second Printing, 2004

Distributed by MorningStar Publications, Inc., a division of MorningStar Fellowship Church
P.O. Box 440, Wilkesboro, NC 28697

International Standard Book Number: 1-929371-43-8

MorningStar's website: www.morningstarministries.org
For information call 1-800-542-0278.

Cover Design by Micah Davis
Book Layout by Sharon Whitby

Unless otherwise indicated, all Scripture quotations are taken from the New American Standard Bible, copyright © 1960, 1962, 1963, 1968, 1971, 1973, 1974, 1977 by The Lockman Foundation. Italics in Scripture are for emphasis only.

# CONTENTS

# INTRODUCTION

ONE OF THE MOST IMPORTANT EVENTS at the end of the church age will be the restoration of the apostolic ministry to the church. The ministry that opened the church age will be the one that closes it. The raising up of a victorious church, demonstrating for all time to all of creation that truth will prevail over lies and righteousness will prevail over iniquity, will be the completed job of the apostolic ministry.

The devil has had a boast since the fall of man—he declares that God's special creation, which He made in His own image, loves evil more than righteousness. Satan proclaims that those whom the Lord created to become members of His family will gladly serve him, the devil, rather than God. He points out that even though God put man in a perfect environment, with perfect conditions, man chose sin and death over living in obedience to God. At the end of this age the church will prove the fallacy of this boast.

At the end of this age the church will live in an imperfect environment in the darkest of times, against the greatest onslaught of evil and temptation, yet she will choose righteousness over iniquity. This will even be a witness to principalities and powers that truth will ultimately prevail over every lie. For this reason even the angelic majesties will declare for eternity that these faithful ones, who were obedient against such an onslaught, are worthy to rule with the Lamb. This is our hope and our purpose—to live lives that glorify the ways of the Lord and prove the power of His goodness over evil.

When a city is rebuilt after its destruction by war or natural disaster, the restored city is more of a marvel and testimony than the previous one. The nature God created mankind with has likewise been almost completely reduced to rubble. However, it will be rebuilt. The main business of the Lord is redemption and then restoration. The church is composed of those who are in this process, who are growing in the grace, power, and nature of the Lord.

However, the church cannot grow to its full stature, or accomplish its full purpose, without the apostolic ministry. Neither can any of the other ministries given to the church grow to their full stature, nor accomplish their full purpose, without the apostolic ministry. We must also understand that the apostolic ministry cannot accomplish its purpose without the other equipping ministries given to the church, which is clearly stated in Ephesians 4:11-13:

> **And He gave some as apostles, and some as prophets, and some as evangelists, and some as pastors and teachers,**
>
> **for the equipping of the saints for the work of service, to the building up of the body of Christ;**
>
> **until we all attain to the unity of the faith, and of the knowledge of the Son of God, to a mature man, to the measure of the stature which belongs to the fulness of Christ.**

The apostle Paul clearly states here that these five equipping ministries are given to the church *"until we*

[1] **all attain to the unity of the faith, and of** [2] **the knowledge of the Son of God,** [3] **to a mature man,** [4] **to the measure of the stature which belongs to the fulness of Christ."** Is there a church anywhere on the earth that has yet attained this stature? We would have certainly heard if this had been attained by a church. Therefore, we obviously still need these ministries that were given to the church—all of them.

This is not a new revelation. The fastest growing part of the church over the last two decades has been what is now being called "the new apostolic movement." Not only does it now appear that a majority of Pentecostal, Charismatic Christians are embracing this truth, but many evangelical, and even those who are often referred to as "old line" denominations, are now embracing it. Where this is happening there is an obvious, new, spiritual energy and excitement created that is helping church life in the twenty-first century become what God intended it to be.

Embracing the truth for the need of equipping ministries seems to bring great blessing and growth, but like all previous restoration movements it has come with controversy, extremes, and mistakes. This should not discourage us. Like the apostle Peter, those with the faith and courage to step out of the boat and start walking on water will also be prone to making some mistakes. As both the Scriptures and church history testify, those who want to walk with God without making any mistakes need not apply. Even so, these also testify that those who do not acknowledge the mistakes for what they are and learn from them are doomed to increasingly worse tragedies.

With the faith and courage to keep pressing on, we also need the wisdom and humility to examine the teachings and practices that are causing unnecessary problems. However, this book is not written for the purpose of examining the present apostolic movements, but rather to help define what true, apostolic ministry is and what the fruit of this ministry should be, which is true, apostolic, church life.

From a perspective of church history after the first century, all of the equipping ministries given to the church were gradually, but generally, removed from the life of the church. I say "generally" because there were many who functioned in these ministries for several more centuries, even if they did not continue to be called by them. There have also been students of history who have made a good case for all of the equipping ministries continuing in the life of the church throughout the church age, but almost entirely in the underground, persecuted church. There is merit to this view, but looking at a broader picture of the church, it appears obvious that all of the ministries were removed in their authority and function in the church in general for over a millennium.

Beginning with The Reformation in the fourteenth century, we see a gradual recovery of these ministries in the reverse order in which they seem to have been lost to the church (I personally mark the beginning of The Reformation with the ministry of John Hus). The first ministry to cease to be recognized by the church, and was therefore lost, was the ministry of the apostle.

It is now clear that this will be the last of these ministries restored, making it the ministry that will have the least amount of time to accomplish its purpose during the church age. Even so, it will be enough. Just as the apostolic church of the first century was the most powerful, and accomplished more for the spread of the gospel than possibly any generation since, the apostolic church at the end will again shake the entire world with its truth and power.

As encouraging as the growing realization of Christians for the need of the apostolic ministry, as well as the other equipping ministries, it is also apparent that we are still quite far from having an authentic apostolic ministry restored. Likewise, it is obvious that the prophetic ministry has not yet truly been restored to the church, and is still in an immature state. In fact, this same thing could be said of all of the equipping ministries.

Just because the pastor, teacher, and evangelist ministries are now widely recognized and accepted throughout the church, and some have been for centuries, this does not mean that they are functioning at the level to which they are called. None of the other ministries given to the church will be fully restored and mature before the apostolic ministry is restored and able to take its place with them.

Without the apostolic ministry, the church will continue to be like a sports team that does not have a coach. They may be gifted players and are able to play, but basically their lack of coordination and discipline will result in a much lower level of performance than they would have with a coach. Such a team will be beaten by teams with far less talent that have a coach. In this same way no ministry in the church can grow to its full stature, or the level of performance and fruitfulness that it could have, without the authority of authentic apostles and elders of the church present.

For most of my Christian life, I have been considered a part of the prophetic ministry and am usually associated with the prophetic movement. I have felt a personal mandate to help see the prophetic ministry restored to its biblical stature and place in the church. When I inquired of the

Lord recently about how much progress we had made, I was surprised when He replied that we were only experiencing about 15 percent to what we are called. That may sound discouraging to some, but it was very encouraging to me. Twenty years ago I would have said it was at about 2 percent, at best.

In this I am not talking about levels of accuracy, but rather the authority and degree of revelation that the prophetic is now walking in compared to what is intended for the New Testament prophetic ministry. Even 2 percent is better than none, but there will be a prophetic ministry raised up by the end that will overshadow any prophetic ministry that has previously walked in this earth. That may sound far-fetched, but it is sound biblical truth. As II Corinthians 3:7-11 states, what we are supposed to experience under the New Covenant should be greater than what was experienced under the Old Covenant. Are there any prophets today who have attained to the stature of what the Old Covenant prophets walked in?

I do know a few, remarkable prophetic ministries that I feel measure up to the biblical stature of this powerful ministry, and a good number more who are growing in authentic prophetic gifts and authority. However, even the most mature and anointed that I know still have a ways to go to even measure up to what was experienced under the Old Covenant. Even so, we can be sure that what Paul wrote in II Corinthians will be proven true before the end of this age—the glory of the New Covenant will greatly overshadow that of the Old.

Like the prophetic ministry at this time, all of the other equipping ministries given to the church are far from what they are called to be. We may think of some extraordinary pastors, teachers, and evangelists, and wonder about the truth of that statement, but I just ask you to consider how much more fruitful they would be if they were in a proper relationship to all of the other equipping ministries. For example, we would not have huge crusades with multitudes "making decisions" with only a tiny percentage of them actually being added to the church. Pastors and teachers would be ready and in place to help these new believers become established in their faith and in the church. No ministry can be what it is called to be, or accomplish all that it is called to accomplish, without being in a proper relationship with the other ministries given to the church. This is the way that the Lord designed His church, and it will not function as He intended without doing it His way.

## THE STATE WE ARE IN

I travel quite extensively, and everywhere I go I try to have at least one meeting just for pastors and leaders of ministries in the country or region. These are usually attended by anywhere from a hundred to a thousand or more. Regardless of the size, I try to use much of the time with the group for questions and answers. For several years now the question that I am most asked is what I think of the new apostolic movements. Usually this is a "loaded question" in which the one asking is at least disturbed, and in some cases, has been deeply offended by them. As I try to get a reading on the others, it is obvious that this is one question that almost everyone seems to have a great interest in at least.

Even though I have my own opinions about them, I always try to share them as just that, also understanding that we "see in part," and **"know in part."** (see I Corinthians

13:12) The following are some things I have seen from inquiring of the Lord. Though I feel He did show me something that is accurate, I still believe all prophetic revelation is still seeing in part. This is the part I was given.

When I inquired of the Lord about the present state of the apostolic ministry, I was shown a number of beautiful, fast looking cars. However, they were not running but were being pushed about by people because they did not have motors. The apostolic movement was also one of these cars, and it was going faster than the others because it had a few more people behind it pushing. What does this mean?

What we have now may look good, and even look fast, but without a lot of human effort it would not be moving at all. This is not only true of the apostolic movement, but it appeared true of all of them. However, as I watched, motors were brought and put in these cars. The motors that came were the apostolic ministries. These did not just come to the apostolic movements, but to the others as well. When they were put in and started, all of the other parts began to function the way for which they were created. When that happens, they are going to not only be able to go fast, but will be able to carry people instead of requiring the people to push them.

As I pondered this, I began to wonder how many churches and movements really exist to equip the people and get them to where they are called to go rather than just using the people to go where they themselves want to go. From my experience, this seemed a very accurate reflection of where the church is in general.

This is not to imply that what has been done to build the church or the present apostolic movements will not be useful. A motor without a car will not do us much good either. Those who are waiting for the car to get its motor before joining it will more than likely wake up one morning and find that the car has left them far behind.

Even so, there is a big difference between what God is empowering and what is being pushed along by human effort. Today the church may have a lot of great looking vehicles, but is their performance really more the result of human effort than the power of God? Motivating people for a purpose is not necessarily wrong, but the apostolic ministry is much more than the ability to motivate people or even to lead people. The apostolic ministry has much more to do with releasing the power of God and empowering people with the authority and power of God in which they are called to walk, rather than it is getting people to follow them.

For this reason much (not all) of what is today called "apostolic" is in fact the exact opposite of the authentic apostolic. Just because someone is a good motivator, a good recruiter, or a good administrator does not make him an apostle. We only have true spiritual authority to the degree that the King Himself lives in us and expresses Himself through us.

## A ROOT PROBLEM

Now I will share something from our experience with the new apostolic movements, again knowing that this is only part of the picture, but it is a part that could have major implications for the future.

I help to oversee a fellowship of churches. We have received many reports from them about how they have been recruited by "apostolic networks." One of them testified to having been recruited by eight different apostolic networks in just one year. This little congregation did eventually go with one of these, which I thought was the right thing for them to do. I had told this pastor if he ever felt any other group could help him more than we could then he was not only free to change his association, but we would bless it and help the transition in any way that we could. I sincerely believed this particular congregation would be served better by such a network than we could serve them at the time. However, such tactics for growing a network reveals some fundamental issues that are decidedly un-apostolic, and that will at some point certainly become major problems.

The New Testament apostles were obviously devoted to helping each other. Paul expressed the desire not to build on another man's foundation, and obviously tried not to do it except when requested. It is fundamental to a true apostolic mentality to be seeking to take new territory for the kingdom. It is also fundamental to a true apostolic mentality to have a vision for the whole body of Christ— not just one's own ministry. Recruiting people or movements from other churches or movements will create divisions, and certainly does not demonstrate a heart for the whole body of Christ.

Even sports teams have the integrity to ask other programs for permission to talk to their players, coaches, or other personnel before trying to hire them. We should be even more devoted to such courtesy in the body of Christ, and those who are not selfishly ambitious will. The recruiting mentality of many of the apostolic movements reveals a serious poverty of spirit, not the Holy Spirit. This rose up in the Shepherding Movement of the seventies that quickly became one of the most divisive and destructive movements of the twentieth century. How is this so destructive?

Right behind the mentality that would motivate one to recruit or take from that which has been the work of others is a control spirit that will ultimately do much damage. This is because what is built on selfish ambition and the strength of the flesh will have to be maintained by the flesh, which is the basic food of the control spirit, as well as every other evil thing as we are told in James 3.

## A WARNING

Years before the apostolic networks became popular, we were given a prophetic warning of a false apostolic movement that would come. I say "we" because this came to several on our team in various ways. We were also told the location where this movement would arise. When I began to inquire about this, I was told that this false apostolic movement would end up being more devastating to the church than the Shepherding Movement had been, and that it would be taken over by the same control spirit and political spirit that came into the Shepherding Movement. The political spirit is what would motivate one to build the church or their ministry more on human alliances than in obedience to the Holy Spirit. From this time, I began more of an in-depth study on these strongholds that resulted in much of what I have written about them since.

At the time these warnings came, there did not seem to be anything in the church that even remotely fit the description of this false apostolic movement. Now there does seem to be some, and it is falling into the pattern of what we were shown. We have been very public about this warning for years. I believe we have shared these warnings every time we have felt to prophetically speak about the restoration of the apostolic ministry to the church.

Obviously, I could not address this subject without bringing up this warning. However, when we are given warnings like this we do not believe that they have to come to pass. We feel that warnings are given to us to help prevent them from coming to pass. That remains our devotion, and is why I feel that I should address what is not apostolic as well as trying to sow a vision for the coming, true apostolic. Also, I have never met a false teacher or false prophet when I did not recognize the calling of God on their life, but had turned to evil or carnal means for gaining influence which opened the door for their corruption.

It seems that there is almost always a "Saul" before there is a "David," when it comes to anything the Lord is restoring to the church. In relation to the establishment of the kingdom in Israel, the Lord had promised Israel a king through Jacob (see Genesis 49:10). It was nearly time for the king to arise and to prepare the people for their coming king when the Lord put the desire in their hearts for a king. However, they could not wait for God's king to mature but demanded a king immediately. By doing this, they rejected God and His provision for them.

So the Lord gave them a king and even anointed him. I think the Lord is doing the same to much of what is being called apostolic today. I also think it is more the people's apostolic ministry than the Lord's, but He listens to His bride and will often give her what she persists in asking for.

Just as Saul fought some of the battles of the Lord and accomplished some things for Israel, he was not able to carry the weight of this responsibility as a king for long. Soon he was attacking anyone else who was anointed, and jealousy began to drive him more than the purpose of God. His ensuing poor leadership caused more problems for the

Lord's king, who was a true king after the Lord's heart. However, David possibly would not have been the great king that he was without the trials provided for him by Saul. Even so, Saul's administration caused many unnecessary problems for Israel, and made it much more difficult for the people to recognize David's anointing to be king.

This is the warning that I was personally given about the restoration of the apostolic ministry to the church— that one would come first that did seem to be "head and shoulders" above the other movements in the church, but it was premature and would cause many problems. Though these biblical precedents are seldom completely accurate in the way they reflect later parallels, they are good guidelines.

We can expect some of those movements today that are called "apostolic" to accomplish some good by fighting some of the battles of the Lord. However, they will also help to mature the true apostolic which is coming, but will cause many problems, making it difficult for Christians in general to recognize the real when it comes.

As stated, this book was not written to debunk teachings or movements, but rather to help prepare the way for the real that is coming. However, I could not call myself a shepherd if I did not try to protect God's people from attacks. I could not call myself a watchman if I did not sound the alarm when I am able to see the danger. Even so, I do not expect a single book to bring an end to the rising controversy surrounding the restoration of the apostolic ministry, and I am not writing this book for that purpose.

Though I have been identified with the prophetic movement for many years, I started teaching on the apostolic ministry long before I ever taught on the prophetic ministry, beginning nearly thirty years ago. I wrote about the apostolic ministry in our original newsletters before I wrote on the prophetic ministry. This is a subject that I have considered not only important, but crucial for the church in our times to understand. I also think that one of the primary purposes of the prophetic ministry is to help prepare the way for the coming apostolic ministry to be fully restored to the church. We cannot experience true New Testament church life as it was intended to be without it.

I also want to say that in spite of all that I have written about the movements, which may end up causing trouble for the church, I have a very high regard for those who have the courage to press beyond the present limits of church life to seek more for the body of Christ. I think some may have carried things a little too far in trying to see the apostolic ministry restored to the church prematurely. They are so full of zeal for the Lord and His people that the devil simply could not stop them. So, he got behind them and pushed them too far. I am also convinced that what the devil intends to do with these can be changed, and I still hold to that. Regardless of the amount of confusion that comes by some prematurely trying to walk in the apostolic ministry, clarity will come and the truth will prevail.

## THE VICTORY IS SURE

An authentic apostolic ministry will be restored to the church. There is abundant evidence that those who will be true apostles in the end times are already among us and are maturing. Like King David, most are faithful shepherds who have learned to fight the lion and bear and will risk their own lives to do this to protect the sheep. They are also probably not regarded highly by their own brothers at this time, but in due time they will be recognized. Even if a prophet comes to pour oil on them and tell them about their high calling, their response to this will be to go back and faithfully watch over the flock they have been given. They will consider if this is from God, they can wait for God to promote them in His time.

In all of these matters, let us keep in mind that there is a ditch on either side of the path of life. If we overreact to extremes on one side, we will fall into the ditch on the other side. It is my prayer for you that this book will help to clarify some things, but even more than that, impart a vision and an understanding for the coming apostolic ministry. It will be far more powerful, and far more exciting, than anything we have yet experienced. These are the times that even the prophets of old desired to see, and you are here!

For those who read this and feel called to this ministry, remember that even King David was willing to serve in the house of Saul. He also refused to lift his hand against **"the Lord's anointed" (I Samuel 26:11).** David could have killed Saul and he could have taken the authority to which the prophet had already told him he was called. Because of this awesome respect that he had for the anointing and for authority, the Lord could trust him with more anointing and more authority than He could have otherwise.

If there is one phrase that rings over and over concerning the apostolic ministry in the book of Acts, it is that they were **"filled with the Spirit."** Possibly the most basic characteristic of those who were true apostles is that they followed the Holy Spirit, which is what I have tried to do in writing this book. I pray that you will do the same in reading it.

Please do keep in mind that I am not by any means claiming to have the whole picture, but am just offering my part of this very important issue. Also, because I know many people skip over introductions, some of the things written here are repeated in the text of the book, so please excuse them.

# CHAPTER ONE

# THE GREATEST POWER ON EARTH

THERE IS MORE POWER IN A SINGLE CHRISTIAN than in all of the armies on the face of the earth. This truth will become known throughout the earth before the end of this age. God dwells in His people, and when His people come to know this as living truth rather than doctrine, the world will then know this truth also.

The emerging generation has been infected with a desire for the supernatural. The most popular books, movies, and television shows almost all deal with supernatural powers. Most of these are attempts to attract people to sorcery and other forms of evil, but the Lord is going to use this for His own purpose.

Man was created to have fellowship with God, who is Spirit and supernatural. Consequently, there is an innate desire within every human being for the supernatural. C.S. Lewis once remarked, *"...spiritual nature, like bodily nature, will be served; deny it food and it will gobble poison."* If man is not restored to his right relationship with God, the desire for the supernatural will be filled with the devil's counterfeits.

Years ago, studies were done that indicated more than twelve billion dollars a year were being spent on psychics in America. An even more shocking aspect of this study was that it appeared more than half of the people calling these psychics claimed to be evangelical Christians. The prophetic gifts that the Lord has given to His church are far greater than anything the devil has, but if you deny children their food they are going to eat something, and it will likely be very bad. This is a tragedy, but it will not continue. The Lord has provided for His people, and He is going to raise up shepherds who will lead them to it.

The power He has already given to His church is much greater than anything Satan can duplicate with his counterfeits. When the church awakens to the power that the Lord has given to her, even the wildest imaginations in Hollywood will not be able to compete with the reality that God's people are going to experience. Just as the multitudes flocked to Jesus, the multitudes are going to come to the church which walks in what God has given to her, giving the people true bread from heaven.

The emerging generation must have adventure in their lives. The devil often takes advantage of this need, but God put it there for a reason. The final generations on this earth are going to live the greatest adventure the world has ever known. There is no greater adventure than the true Christian life, and the true Christian life is about to be restored to the earth. This true and ultimate adventure is food for the soul. Many try to meet this need with movies and books through which they try to live vicariously, but none of these can ever fully satisfy our longing for this reality in our lives. There is nothing that can satisfy this longing like the true Christian life.

We must also understand that this will mean the end of the church as it is now. Radical change is coming. Those who are not discerning enough to see it and become a part of it will not survive much longer. This is not a slam against the church as it is, which has been effective in its time, and a powerful salt and light in the earth in its generations. The church is also the mother of the great, last day ministry which is soon to emerge. However, just as Rachel died giving birth to Benjamin (see Genesis 35:16-19), the last son born to Israel, the same will happen to the church when the last day ministry is born.

We must keep in mind that few biblical types or models fit perfectly with what they are intended to represent. They are parables which are intended to teach us. So, just as the Lord is not coming back for literal sheep and goats, we must understand that parables and types have their limits. At the same time, we must always keep in mind that the church is the Lord's bride. It is nearing the end of the church age and He is coming back for the bride who has been called, is prepared, and is worthy of Him. A major part of the church as we know it is not going to die because it has failed, but because it has succeeded. It will have brought to birth the ministry that will help the world transition between the church age and the kingdom age.

When Benjamin was born his mother tried to name him Ben-oni, which means "son of my sorrows" (see Genesis 35:18). She named him this because she knew she was dying. However, Israel changed his name to Benjamin, which means "son of the right hand." The right hand of God is where Jesus sits, which in Matthew 26:64 is called "the right hand of power." Benjamin, the last son born to Israel, represents the last day ministry, the last sons to be born on the earth. With that generation, the church age will have closed because the number of those who are called to rule and reign with Christ as members of His own family will have been completed.

The Laodicean church was the last of the seven churches that the Lord addressed in the book of Revelation, which also represents the last day church. The Scriptures say this church was so rich that they did not think they needed anything and were therefore lukewarm, so the Lord vomited them out (see Revelation 3:14-16). However, we need also to recognize that the promises to the overcomers of this church were the greatest promises given to any church. The overcomers of the Laodicean church in Revelation were promised to sit with the Lord on His throne (see Revelation 4:21). This is in contrast to the **"great multitude"** who stand **"before the throne" (Revelation 7:9).**

Having as much as we do in the natural in these times may be the most difficult thing to overcome in order to keep our zeal and devotion to the Lord. But, those who do are trusted with the greatest authority. They will demonstrate the authority of Jesus, who He is and where He sits because they will be seated with Him. To walk in this they must learn what it means to buy from Him gold purified in the fire and the white garments of purity (see Revelation 3:14-22).

Basically, that is what this book is about. It is for those who will pay the price for the pure gold and walk in the purity of life that is befitting the sons and daughters of the King, **" for many are called, but few are chosen" (Matthew 22:14).** Many want to walk in all that we are discussing, but there are not many willing to pay the price to get there. Everyone wants to do the fun stuff, but very few want to endure the discipline, the scourging, and give the focused devotion that is required to be proven trustworthy.

We are living in the Laodicean times when almost everything comes so easily that it is truly a rare soul who can rise above this to pursue the true gold and the white garments. But those who do may be the most trustworthy of all. Everyone gets excited when we speak prophetically of the wonderful things that are about to happen on the earth. People start to sit on the edge of their seats as we speak of these things; some even stand on their seats cheering. However, when it comes to the practical teaching about the discipline required to actually walk in these things, many of the same people start to nod off into sleep or drift out into the hall.

However, not all drift away like this. There are rare souls in every audience who are just as keen to learn what will help them walk in their purpose. They usually have their notebooks out, and you can tell that they do not want to miss a single word. Then they go home and review their notes, planning and seeking ways to walk out what they have learned. They are the good soil which will bear fruit with the seeds that are planted in them.

I have a number of friends who are, or have been, all pro athletes. I have talked with some of them about the focus and discipline to which they gave themselves for many years to get where they are. Before becoming teenagers, they gave hours every single day to training, building themselves up, practicing, and learning from others who had been successful before them. I have heard some of them say that they know many who are more talented than they are, possibly in every city where they play. But, they are sitting in the stands watching them and dreaming about playing instead of playing simply because they did not have the discipline and focus it took to make it to that level.

If these guys can give that kind of devotion to a game, how much more devoted should we be to making our calling and election sure in Christ? As Paul the apostle pointed out concerning athletes, they run for a **"perishable wreath"** (see I Corinthians 9:24-25), but we are running for one which is eternal! To be called as an emissary of the King of kings is the highest calling that one can have on this earth. If we do not want our place in Christ more than an athlete wants his place on a team, then we certainly are not worthy of such a position.

## DISCERN THE THIEF

One of the biggest thieves in the church today is called "the easy way," which is the same temptation Satan used to tempt the Lord Jesus. He promised Jesus if He would just bow down and worship him he would give Him the kingdoms of this world (see Matthew 4:8-9). Jesus was already promised these, but what Satan was tempting Him with was to be able to get them the easy way, without going to the cross. This same temptation is still used against all who are called and many fall to it.

Recently, an investment scheme was exposed that had bilked churches and ministries out of hundreds of millions of dollars. This is the second time this has happened in just the last few years. Some churches and ministries actually fell to both of these. Both came with the same calling card: "The wealth of the wicked is about to be given to the righteous." This is biblical and will come true. However, you will find throughout the Scriptures that wealth is given to the diligent—it will not come through "get rich quick" schemes.

The last scheme promised a 40 percent return on invest-ments each month from income generated through imports. Having been in business, I know the only kind of imports which can generate even close to that kind of return are not legal. When I asked some of those who had invested in this latest scheme if they had asked what the imports were, I could only find one who had asked and he could not find out anything, but he still invested!

It seems there were not any illegal imports associated with this latest sham because there were no imports at all. It was just a big pyramid scheme. Hundreds of millions of dollars in kingdom resources were lost, again. The Lord is not worried about these losses because He has an unlimited supply, but I think He is concerned about what makes His people, even some of His most influential and visible leaders, fall to this trap.

The mask the thief wears is the "easy way," the "quick way," the "painless way," and does not require much on our part. I read one study which indicated that two-thirds of Americans included as the main factor in their retirement plan to win a lottery. These are the ones who are likely to be working for those who had discipline and focused vision until the day they die . The ones who do enjoy a comfortable retirement will be those who invested faithfully and wisely in their plans year after year.

The Scriptures indicate that quick riches are a curse, not a blessing. Have you read the studies on those who won lotteries? Has there been a single one yet who has been found to be better off just five years later, or even two? Most seem to not only end up broke again in a short period of time, but very bitter, wounded, or worse.

When I heard about one man winning who was already a very successful businessman and obviously a Christian who immediately tithed from his winnings, I confess to thinking that for the first time maybe someone had won that would really benefit from it and benefit the kingdom. Then a report came on the news concerning the state to which this man seemed to have fallen, and it was most discouraging.

I have a number of famous, highly successful and easily recognizable friends from professional sports and entertainment. I have walked down the hall of a hotel and watched shoeshine boys spot them and immediately ask for a loan of fifty thousand dollars. I was shocked and began asking my friends how often this happens. Usually the response is "every day." Many are now hated by family members and former friends because they would not give them the large sums of money for which they asked. They are scorned for "abandoning their roots" in the inner cities, but they cannot even go there anymore without continual demands for money. This harassment quickly turns to anger and even rage when the money is not given.

As I am the leader of a fairly successful ministry, I also know how this feels to a degree. It is rare when I mix with new people that I am not bombarded with requests to publish their books or listen to their vision. They want me to use the platform that it took me decades to build to promote theirs into happening more quickly for them.

The request which amuses me the most is the one for me to lay hands on people and impart my writing gift. It took me forty years of discipline, staying home, and working hard while others played to do what I do, and they want me to impart this to them with a single touch! I have met many,

many people who think the key to them having a successful ministry is getting a book published. For those who think like that, such a thing would probably be as devastating as winning the lottery.

Now my complaint here is certainly not true for all, but I confess to longing for the time when the conversation of most Christians will be about the great things the Lord is doing, instead of the great things they are doing or even intending to do "for the Lord."

It is okay to be immature when you are young. It is right for an infant to be self-centered because they are so helpless that they are not yet capable of even thinking in terms of how they might help others, much less do it. However, if someone is twenty years old and still has to wear a diaper, there is a problem. One of the Lord's warnings concerning the last days was **"woe to those who are nursing babies in those days" (Matthew 24:19).** Interpret that, "Woe to those who keep their people in immaturity."

We are far from apostolic Christianity. Those who are most presumptuous in claiming to be there by taking the apostolic mantel seem to be the most immature of all. I rejoice in the courage of anyone who would press beyond the limits of our times and pursue the apostolic faith, but we cannot accept cheap substitutes.

The word that is translated "faith" in the New Testament is also translated "faithfulness." I do think these words are interchangeable. Faithfulness may be the greatest and truest test of true faith. As we are told in Hebrews 6:11-12:

> **And we desire that each one of you show the same diligence so as to realize the full assurance of hope until the end,**

**that you may not be sluggish, but imitators of those who through faith and patience inherit the promises.**

As this Scripture indicates, it will require diligence to realize our **"full assurance"** at the end. As I have lamented, often publicly, if it takes **"faith and patience"** to inherit the promises, why do we have this huge "faith movement," but no one has even heard of a "patience movement?" No doubt, patience would not draw nearly the crowds or sell nearly as many books. However, for those who will actually inherit the promises it is just as much of a devotion.

I intend to sow some prophetic vision in this book. I will impart most of it in the middle of the teachings on biblical character and discipline, which we will be required to walk in for what is to come. I have been repeatedly told that if I would just write the vision, I would distribute many more books. I need to make it clear now that it is never my goal to sell a lot of books. My target audience is not the ones who tend to buy books, but the ones who I think are going to bear fruit. They will rejoice as much in the practical as they will the visions. It takes these to make true champions in any field. Some of the greatest champions of the faith who have ever walked the earth are now alive and are being awakened to their purposes.

Some of those I am writing for are not even eight years old yet, and some of them are over eighty. Age is not what they have in common. The main thing they have in common are the ears which can hear the sound of the trumpet and hearts which are drawn to the sound of battle.

I trust that for you to have this book in your hand and to have gone this far, you are one of these. We will discuss many exciting things and many hard things, but to the wise they are both interesting and crucial.

My goal is not literary excellence, but to sow seed, water it, and see it bear fruit in real lives. Therefore I will be redundant and I will do it shamelessly. I have borrowed heavily from previous books and articles I have written, as well as my spoken messages. If you are one of those who have complained about this, please understand that I am doing this on purpose. I also confess to appreciating those who have made such complaints, as I at least know you are reading carefully enough to notice. I pray that the continual pounding of some of these things will get through.

A physician friend, Dr. Grimes, recently told me that thoughts travel by electrical impulses in our brains and then through our nervous system, which has of course been known for a long time. However, he said studies have also shown that a new idea must be repeated an average of twenty-nine times to create a neural "pathway" or "bridge," which means it then becomes a part of our thinking.

I have read other studies that said new ideas have to be heard an average of four times just to be retained and thirty times or more to become a belief which changes our thinking, verifying what Dr. Grimes told me. The renewing of our mind is a much slower, more tedious matter than many want to consider. This is why the Bible itself is so redundant, repeating many lessons over and over. This is also why *successful* athletes go through the same drills and workouts over and over for the entire time they remain successful athletes in their sport.

One factor I have found to be in the character with every person who has enjoyed significant success in their life is that they did not waste their time. A second factor that I have found to be in every great leader I have met is that they seem addicted to books on leadership. Some have said that they read at least a chapter a day from one. Most read at least three or four books a year. You would think there is not that much which can be said about the subject and you are right. They are mostly reading the same things said in different ways. However, this is how their minds are fashioned to do what they do and to keep them on course.

I heard one man say that his wife had prepared him literally thousands of meals, and he could only remember a handful as being truly outstanding, but all the others sustained him! The same is true with food for our soul. We may only read a few books or hear a few sermons which are truly outstanding, but the rest are just as necessary to sustain us.

I am saying this to encourage you that when you read something you have read before or heard somewhere else, do not skip over it—pray over it. Let it sink in a little deeper. Ask the Lord to water the seed and He will—over and over. This is required if you are going to be doers of the Word, bear fruit, and accomplish the purpose for which you are now on the earth.

You are called to reveal the greatest power on earth, by living the greatest life on earth. Do not ever forget this. Repeat it to yourself every day. Determine every day that it will not be wasted, but everything that happens is a part of your training. Seize the opportunity. You will come alive, and the power of life will begin to flow through you. Seize the day!

# CHAPTER TWO

# A GLORIOUS QUEST

WE ARE COMING TO THE MOST EXCITING TIMES that there have ever been upon the earth. These are the times that the prophets and wise men of old desired to see—and you are here. This is an unfathomable privilege. The **"great cloud of witnesses" (Hebrews 12:1)** really are watching you. They are the faithful ones who have gone before us, whose labors helped to make what you are called to walk in possible.

We may wonder how it could ever have been better than to have walked with Jesus when He was on the earth. However, He Himself said that it was better for Him to go away so that the Holy Spirit could come (see John 16:7). When the Holy Spirit came to His people, they did not have Him in the flesh—they had Him living inside of them! What is coming upon the world in the last days is the result of Christians waking up to the reality of the One who lives within them.

This is our quest, to live in the reality of Who lives in us. To live in this reality there are clear principles outlined in the Scriptures. This is the foundation in which every truly successful life is built upon. True success is doing our Creator's will. It is to finish our course, to have used the talents that He entrusted to us, and then to hear on that great day, **"Well done good and faithful servant" (Matthew 25:21 NIV).** To stand in His glorious presence on that awesome day and hear those words will be far greater than any human achievement that we could ever have attained on the earth. To not hear them will be the greatest failure, the greatest tragedy of all. But you have been appointed for the glory and success of being obedient and faithful.

The reason the church emerged in the book of Acts as a force that could so change the world was because the Lord was among them. They had encounters with Him day by day. He was their message and He did great works among them. Because of this it was not long before the most powerful potentates on the planet knew of these people, and not long afterward, were in great fear of them. These believers shook the earth with their message and their lives. It will happen again.

It seems as if the Lord purposely chose leaders for His new church that absolutely no one would follow unless they were anointed with His presence. The people knew that those who now stood before them as their leaders had almost all recently denied the Lord and fled from Him when He needed them the most. These leaders did not have a great plan or program. In fact, there was no reason for anyone to follow them, except one—the Lord had appointed them and He had anointed them. Their authority was the result of just one fact—the King lived in them.

The first century church really had only one thing going for them—God. He was all that they would need. The Lord was in their midst, living, doing wonders, teaching, comforting, and providing. There is no other way that what happened can be explained. No one would follow fishermen, tax gatherers, and peasants who had proven to be faithless and undependable unless the Lord was with them, which He was, mightily.

The Lord had His first leaders in a place where they were completely dependent on Him. They could not lead, build, or even teach unless He was present. They had no other plan to fall back on if He did not go with them and do the works. If the Lord did not go with them they were helpless. The church is about to return to this same foundation.

What good is the most glorious temple if God is not in it? If He is in it, it will not be the temple that captures your attention, regardless of how glorious it is. The church will soon return to its purpose of being the dwelling place of God on the earth.

The first four words in the Bible are the most important in the Bible—*"In the beginning God..."* (Genesis 1:1). The church began in such a way that this was an unquestionable reality. This lasted for a time and then one could say concerning the history of the church: *"after the beginning...man."* The new creation, the church, started as a dwelling place for God. The most important thing that had been lost by the Fall, man's intimacy with God, had been restored. The veil of the temple had been rent and all could approach Him, know Him, walk with Him, and be His very dwelling place. Then the church also chose to eat of the forbidden fruit, just as the bride of the first Adam had done. Then she started looking at herself, trying to cover herself while actually hiding from His presence, substituting rituals for the truths they represented.

Even so, the Lord foresaw this, spoke of it through His prophets, and promised that even though the bride of **"the last Adam" (I Corinthians 15:45)** had also fallen, she would be restored, and restored she would rule with Him. This restoration has now been going on for hundreds of years, and though progress has been made it seems if we keep the same timeline, many hundreds more will be required to complete the job. However, there is another factor—the Lord is going to suddenly come into His temple. In His manifest presence everything will change—fast!

## WE MUST BE BORN AGAIN, AGAIN

It is now time for the church to be born again, again. We must return to our beginning. Many have been hearing this call for years, but have often interpreted it as we need to return to the *way* the first century church did things. Of course there is much merit to that, but more than returning to the way things were done, we must return to the One who does the works. The Lord is going to insist on building His own house.

If the Lord really showed up and began to do the building in most of our congregations, it would ruin many of our present programs. One friend of mine used to start his sermons with, "Well, if the Lord does not show up today we have a pretty good program anyway." This was shocking to many who heard it, but I think much more honest than what most of us do, which is tying to claim that what *we* do is God.

We have become very skillful at keeping the people entertained and occupied, believing that God is doing many things which honestly He would not touch. This is what the Lord meant when He spoke through Jeremiah.

**My people have become lost sheep; their shepherds have led them astray. They have made them turn aside on the mountains; they have gone along from mountain to hill and have forgotten their resting place (Jeremiah 50:6).**

This is probably the most frequent way the Lord's people have been "led astray" since the beginning—going **"from mountain to hill,"** from hype to hype, from one thing that pumps them up to the next. They are always moving, but are never being led to their resting place, which is a relationship to the Lord Himself. This is a primary reason for much of the lukewarmness which permeates the church today. The people are simply weary from all of the hype and projects that are forced upon them which are not of God. They signed up for the Lord, but somehow all they ever get is us! We have tried to build the church on almost everything but the only Foundation that will ever hold— the Lord Jesus Himself. Now we have abundant evidence that this will never work.

In Revelation 3:20 we have the amazing scene of the Lord on the outside of His church knocking, wanting to come in. He is a Gentleman and He will not force Himself upon His bride. Building on the foundation of Jesus is much more than just teaching about Him. It is even more than just inviting Him in. It is letting Him do the building (see Hebrews 3:3-6).

In this day when we have so much that will attract people, it is difficult to build something in utter dependence on God. We can provide a pretty good program without Him, and it does not take nearly as much faith. There are proven strategies that will bring the people in. All we have to do is follow the instructions and they will come. But will He?

During the Middle Ages, one of the great leaders of the church was walking with a friend who was pointing out the glories of their city cathedral to him. Observing the great treasures of the church, the friend remarked that the church could no longer say, "Silver and gold have I none." To this his companion replied, "And neither can we say, 'In the name of Jesus rise up and walk.'"

The first century church had abundant evidence of the Lord's presence with them. Almost everything they did was far beyond human ingenuity or brilliance. In fact, the first century church did not leave any buildings or programs behind. They only left transformed lives, families, and even nations.

The Lord has blessed many great works and movements, and He has even occasionally visited a few with His manifest presence. Even so, rare are the churches of which it could be said, "the Lord dwells in them." Is this not our quest, to find the city that God is building, the place where He wants to dwell? What would the church look like if it were built not to attract people, but to attract God?

II Corinthians 3:7-8 is one of the most challenging texts in the New Testament: **"But if the ministry of death, in letters engraved on stones, came with glory, so that the sons of Israel could not look intently at the face of Moses because of the glory of his face, fading as it was, how shall the ministry of the Spirit fail to be even more with glory?"** By this Paul was saying that the glory we are supposed to be experiencing in the New Covenant is even greater than what Moses experienced—Moses had to put a veil over his face because the glory emanating from him was so great it scared people! Do you know anyone who has walked in that kind of glory?

The apostles to the first century church did walk in a remarkable glory and manifest presence of the Lord. In Acts 5:15, we see when just the shadow of Peter touched people they were healed. When Paul's handkerchiefs touched people they were healed. The things done by them were so extraordinary that when Paul and Silas limped into a city, the authorities of the most powerful empire in the world trembled, lamenting that those who had turned the world upside down had come to their city. Even the demons declared, **"I recognize Jesus, and I know about Paul... (Acts 19:15).** These apostles were known throughout the world, and throughout hell, but even more importantly, they were known in heaven.

Even so, as extraordinary as the first century church was, it could be argued that they did not experience more glory than Moses. However, before this age ends, the glory of the New Covenant will be proven to be a greater glory than anything experienced under the Old Covenant. I wrote years ago that a time was coming when even children would lay hands on hospital buildings and everyone inside would be healed. I have recently heard credible reports of this happening in small villages in some third world countries. For this I rejoice, but I know it is just the beginning. We will see this happen with major hospitals in major world-class cities, and the whole world will know about it.

The prophets under the Old Covenant were known even throughout the heathen nations around Israel. It was told to their kings that nothing could be hidden from these prophets, even what the kings spoke in their innermost chambers. Before the end comes this will likewise be said again by the world's rulers—there is nothing they can say or do that is hidden from God's prophets.

There were prophets under the Old Covenant who were very surprised when anything happened that they did not foresee, thinking the Lord had hidden it from them for some reason. Today we are still closer to the place where we tend to be surprised when we do foresee major events, but the time is coming when there will be a prophetic ministry which no person or event could ever sneak up on. The eyes of His body will see with His eyes—everything.

Under the Old Covenant, prophets called down fire from heaven to prove the God they served, consuming those who threatened them (see II Kings 1). Before the end of this age, prophets will again call down fire from heaven to prove the One they serve, but it will be to save the souls of those who threaten them, not destroy them.

Of course the devil will try to counterfeit everything the Lord does. But just as the sorcerers of Egypt ultimately bowed to the power of God and acknowledged His power (see Exodus 8:19), the Lord will show Himself greater than all. Moses destroyed the gods of Egypt, and parted the Red Sea to lead God's people to freedom (see Exodus 14:21). Leaders will again arise to destroy the gods of this world and lead God's people to freedom. Parting the Red Sea will hardly be remembered as a significant miracle after the things that will be done by those who serve the Lord at the end of this age. It will be demonstrated again that the Almighty is in fact all-mighty, and that our King sits above all rule, authority, and dominion.

Moses met with the Lord face to face (see Exodus 33:11). The New Covenant will again trump the Old as the Lord will not just meet face to face with His people—He will dwell in them! There is a leadership that will arise who fully understands the apostolic mandate as Paul stated it in Colossians 1:25-29:

> **Of this church I was made a minister according to the stewardship from God bestowed on me for your benefit, that I might fully carry out the preaching of the word of God,**
>
> **that is, the mystery which has been hidden from the past ages and generations; but has now been manifested to His saints,**
>
> **to whom God willed to make known what is the riches of the glory of this mystery among the Gentiles, which is Christ in you, the hope of glory.**
>
> **And we proclaim Him, admonishing every man and teaching every man with all wisdom, that we may present every man complete in Christ.**
>
> **And for this purpose also I labor, striving according to His power, which mightily works within me.**

The church that is about to emerge at the end of this age will be known for many things, but without question the main thing will be that God is in her. She will heal, deliver, restore, transform, and at times provide for multitudes and multitudes, just as Jesus did when He walked the earth. This church will even do greater works because He has now ascended, and sits above all rule, authority, dominion, and power.

The gospel of the kingdom that He said must be preached in all of the world before the end could come, has not yet been preached (see Matthew 24:14). He is right now preparing the messengers who will do this. This gospel will not come in words alone, but in power that demonstrates it is a kingdom greater than any kingdom has ever been or ever will be. If you are alive today, it is your calling to be a part of this. The hope of our glory, the glory that will reveal Him, is the Christ who is in us. This glory will soon be seen.

Since the first century there have probably always been believers who longed for and prayed for a "book of Acts move of God" to come upon the church again. But what took place in the book of Acts was in a relatively small part of the world and was accomplished by just a handful of believers. If you took all of the extraordinary things that God is presently doing throughout the worldwide church, it would greatly exceed what was written in the book of Acts. Even so, no one can yet say that John 14:12 has been fulfilled, where the Lord said: **"Truly, truly, I say to you, he who believes in Me, the works that I do shall he do also; and greater works than these shall he do; because I go to the Father."** Yet before the end of this age comes, it will be testified that this was certainly true. Even the greatest works that are being done in the world at this time will be accomplished by relatively new believers. The apostles and prophets of the last day church will walk in the power of the age to come.

In 1987, I had a prophetic experience which lasted for two and a half days. In this experience I was given a panoramic vision of a move of God that was much greater than anything I had ever heard before. I saw the greatest ingathering of souls into the kingdom that there had ever been. This has already been fulfilled. Since I wrote the book, *The Harvest,* in which I shared this vision, more people have come to Jesus than all who came from the Day of Pentecost recorded in the book of Acts until 1987.

Certainly, one reason for this is the fact that there are more people alive and on the earth today than have lived on the earth during the entire previous two thousand years. Even so, the greatest harvest that the world has ever known is happening right now. Some studies have estimated that between 200,000 and 400,000 new believers are coming into the kingdom every day, worldwide. Some nations in South and Central America and in Africa estimated that there were times when people were being born again at a rate faster than they were being physically born in those countries.

Great waves of revival are happening in the world today and we can expect them to increase. Even so, I wrote in the book, *The Harvest,* that this was but the first wave I was shown. I saw that this first one would be so great that many would think it was the harvest at the end of the age, but it was not. It was just the ingathering of those who were to be laborers in the harvest which would truly mark the end of this age.

I also wrote that there would be a lull between those two great waves for the purpose of training and equipping those who were called to be laborers in the next great wave. I believe we have actually been in this time for the last decade or so. The next wave is yet to come, but it is easy to feel the swell of the waters and know it is not far away.

# CHAPTER THREE

# HOW DO WE GET THERE?

FOR THE FIRST TWELVE HUNDRED YEARS OF CHURCH history the institutional church that had evolved claimed to be seated upon the seat of Peter. Peter's ministry and message were the main focus of that time and the church reflected it. Spectacular victories were followed by shocking errors. The Reformation really began with a rediscovery of the Epistles of Paul and since then the main emphasis of the church has been the theology of Paul. Paul was unquestionably one of the great builders of the New Testament church. More than anyone else, Paul's theology and revelation set a true course for Christianity. Even so, Paul is not the foundation of the church—Jesus is. Since the Reformation we have used Paul to interpret Jesus rather than the other way around. The true foundations of Christian truth are the teachings of Jesus, not Paul.

This is not to in any way imply that Paul's Epistles do not deserve to be canon Scripture or that they are not true Words from God. It is a matter of where they are to be placed in the building. We will misinterpret and misapply them if they are not rightly built upon the foundation of the teachings of Jesus. Likewise, the teachings of Jesus will be misinterpreted and misapplied if we try to view them through the teachings of anyone else, rather than as the foundation for all other understanding.

Paul's teachings made many great and insightful references to the kingdom of God, but they mostly dealt with the practical issues of the church and some basic issues of doctrine. The church is a part of the kingdom of God, but it is just a part. The Lord's teachings were devoted to the kingdom and only made a couple of references to the church. Unless the church is viewed from this perspective, we will become church-centric rather than Christ-centric.

When the church becomes self-centered, she loses her ability to see the glory of the Lord and to be changed by that glory. She will also have a distorted view of the kingdom and therefore a distorted view of her relationship to the world.

## THE ONE LOAF

Many think of the Gospels as the milk that we give to new believers, and when we mature we go on to the apostolic Epistles. This is a terrible delusion. The greatest depth of revelation that we will ever find in the Bible is found in the Gospels, in the teachings of the Lord Jesus Himself. There is a depth of understanding to be had in every parable and every miracle that we have not yet begun to fathom. John 6 is one of the pivotal chapters in the Bible—one which is especially relevant to us now.

This chapter begins with a great multitude following Jesus because of the signs they saw Him performing (verse 2). It was the time of the Passover and since Jesus was the Passover Lamb sent from God, He would feed the people as a sign. Often overlooked are signs that point to something. Every miracle Jesus did was a message—Jesus fed the five thousand.

After the Lord had gone to the other side of the lake, the people found Him and He rebuked them because they were not following Him for the signs, but because of the food He had given them (see verse 26). He then gave them one of the most important teachings in the Scriptures, declaring that He Himself is the Bread which came down from heaven— if we do not partake of Him, we will not have life. It then says, **"As a result of this many of His disciples withdrew and were not walking with Him anymore" (John 6:66).**

There are many other profound truths in this chapter, but the main point is many follow Him because of the miracles, and many more will follow Him for His provision, but when it comes down to how many are following Him for who He is, there will not be many left.

If we want big crowds to follow our ministry, we can preach either signs and wonders or God's provision and we will probably never be lacking for people. These things are not wrong; they are in fact great biblical truths, but when they become the reason that we are following Him, they become an idol and a false foundation for faith. We want to preach signs and wonders and see God's provision, but above all else, we must know Him and be joined to Him.

Signs and wonders and God's provision are individual truths, but if they are what we are building upon, the day will come when there will not be many left. I believe the loaves that the Lord gave to the people were representative of individual truths. After the people ate of the loaves, what did they have left over? Fragments! Then Jesus explained to them that He is the one Loaf!

We must not continue trying to build the church on individual truths, but on a relationship with Jesus who is the Truth. Only then will we be able to partake of the individual truths and not have them divide us. Any truth that is taken in isolation from His living person will be divisive, as the Scriptures themselves teach.

> **God, after He spoke long ago to the fathers in the prophets in many portions and in many ways,**
>
> **in these last days *has spoken to us in His Son...* (Hebrews 1:1-2).**
>
> **You search the Scriptures because you think that in them you have eternal life; and it is these that bear witness of Me (John 5:39).**
>
> **For as many as may be the promises of God, *IN HIM* they are yes... (II Corinthians 1:20).**
>
> **Now the promises were spoken to Abraham and to his seed. *He does not say, "And to seeds," as referring to many, but rather to one, "And to your seed," that is, CHRIST* (Galatians 3:16 emphasis mine).**

When we take the promises of God individually and not in submission to Him, even they can become idols to distract us from the Tree of Life Himself. None of the promises are made to us as individuals or even as the church, but **"in Him."**

I wrote in my first book, *There Were Two Trees In The Garden,* what I still believe to be one of my most important statements, "The Son of Man is still seeking a place to lay His head, a place where He can be the Head." This was the basic theme of that first book and as I still hear frequently that it was the best book I have written. I confess that I do not know how to measure that, but I think it may have had the most important message of any book I have yet written. I am therefore very encouraged that it remains one of our bestsellers twenty years after I wrote it. Everything is about Jesus, not us. The whole creation is about Him, and the ultimate purpose of God is for all things to be summed up in Him. When we see Him in all things, all things start to make sense.

When we devote ourselves to building a church that attracts God, instead of just something that will attract people, we will at least be starting to go in the right direction. This is our quest, to be a part of the church who has Christ as both the Foundation and the Head. Our goal is not to just establish men in authority, but to establish Christ as authority over men. We must preach the kingdom by exhibiting Jesus as the King.

## THE FIRST STONE IN THE FOUNDATION

Now, to repeat just a bit of what I wrote in my first book, when Jesus was born the only way He could be found was by revelation. The same is still true. In Matthew 16:13-18, we see the first stone laid in the foundation of the church, and the way in which every subsequent stone must be laid.

> **Now when Jesus came into the district of Ceasarea Philippi, He began asking His disciples, saying, "Who do people say that the Son of Man is?"**
>
> **And they said, "Some say John the Baptist; and others, Elijah; but others, Jeremiah, or one of the prophets.**
>
> **He then said to them, "But who do you say that I am?"**

**And Simon Peter answered and said, "Thou art the Christ, the Son of the living God."**

**And Jesus answered and said to him, "Blessed are you, Simon Barjona, because flesh and blood did not reveal this to you, but My Father who is in heaven.**

**And I also say to you that you are Peter** ["a stone"] **and upon this rock** [a large rock or bedrock] **I will build my church; and the gates of Hades shall not overpower it.**

The bedrock the church is built upon is the revelation from the Father. It is not who men say that He is; we each must have our own revelation of Him. We must each have our own well and our own relationship to Him. Probably the main reason Solomon fell after building the temple was he only had his father's vision for that work; he did not have a vision of his own. The strength of every congregation will be dependent upon how strong every individual's personal relationship is to the Lord.

Immediately after Peter expressed his revelation of who Jesus was, they were taken to the Mount of Transfiguration. This is possibly the second most important revelation for those who would be the leaders of the church and for us to have.

**And six days later Jesus took with Him Peter and James and John his brother, and brought them up to a high mountain by themselves.**

**And He was transfigured before them; and His face shone like the sun, and His garments became as white as light.**

And behold, Moses and Elijah appeared to them, talking with Him.

And Peter answered and said to Jesus, "Lord, it is good for us to be here; if You wish, I will make three tabernacles here, one for You, and one for Moses, and one for Elijah."

While he was still speaking, behold, a bright cloud overshadowed them; and behold, a voice out of the cloud, saying, "This is My beloved Son, with whom I am well-pleased; listen to Him!"

And when the disciples heard this, they fell on their faces and were much afraid.

And Jesus came to them and touched them and said, "Arise, and do not be afraid."

And lifting up their eyes, they saw no one, except Jesus Himself alone (Matthew 17:1-8).

The first thing the disciples saw here was the Lord glorified and Moses and Elijah speaking to Him. Moses and Elijah represented the Law and the Prophets, both of which spoke of Him. However, the first response of Peter was to think about building something for this great revelation. Then the Father spoke: **"This is My beloved Son...listen to Him!"** Then they **"fell on their faces and were much afraid."** They badly needed this rebuke, and so do we. The Lord does not want us trying to build on our revelations, not even our revelations of who He is. When a revelation comes our first response must not be to build, but to keep listening—there is much more!

After this rebuke from the Father they lifted up their eyes and **"saw no one except, Jesus Himself alone."** This is the most important revelation we can have. Until we see Him as the whole revelation, as the whole loaf, as the whole purpose of God, we are not ready to build.

## SUMMARY

Because the foundation is crucial, we want to take the time to lay a good foundation for this study. In the next part we will continue our study of the foundation of the church, especially as it is seen in the first century church. Then we will have a grid, or paradigm, from which to understand the rest of history. If we have a right foundation we will also be able to more accurately judge the present state of the church and our own present works. Then we can hold fast to that which is good, and discard that which has proven not to be.

# CHAPTER FOUR

# THE GREAT COMMISSION

TO UNDERSTAND THE CHURCH, ITS HISTORY OR ITS future, we must first understand her mission and message. The foundation for her message and the most clear articulation of her message is seen in the first century church, which is where we will begin this study.

Before His ascension, the Lord gave His apostles a commission that has since been called, and rightly so, "The Great Commission."

**And Jesus came up and spoke to them, saying, "All authority has been given to Me in heaven and on earth.**

**"Go therefore and make disciples of all the nations, baptizing them in the name of the Father and the Son and the Holy Spirit,**

**teaching them to observe all that I commanded you; and lo, I am with you always, even to the end of the age" (Matthew 28:18-20).**

The foundation of the Great Commission is that all authority has been given to Jesus in both heaven and earth. The Great Commission is essentially the proclamation of His authority. The message of the church was not the church. She was not sent forth to establish her own authority, but to proclaim His. For the entire time Jesus walked the earth He only made a couple of very brief mentions of the church. His message was bigger than the church; it was the kingdom of God. When the first century church began to go forth with her message, it was not a message about herself, but about her King.

## CHRIST-CENTRICITY

The apostolic burden was not to bring the church into a certain form, but to see Jesus formed within His people. There is a difference—one is Christ-centered; the other is man-centered. The more church-centric the church became, the more quickly she fell into the prophesied apostasy. For as long as her message remained Christ-centered, she remained pure.

This is not meant in any way to detract from the glory of the church. She is called to be the bride of the King of kings. Her destiny is glorious beyond our comprehension. However, we will never become who we are called to be by looking at ourselves. We will only be changed into who we are called to be as we behold His glory.

**But we all, with unveiled face beholding as in a mirror the glory of the Lord, are being transformed into the same image from glory to glory, just as from the Lord, the Spirit (II Corinthians 3:18).**

The more focused we are on who we are, the less likely we are to fulfill our purpose. One of the greatest distractions to come upon the church has been the *over-emphasis* of who we are in Christ, instead of who He is in us. It is important for us to know who we are called to be, but we will never be who we are called to be as long as this is our primary devotion.

The church became and remained what she had been called to be only as long as she remained faithful to the message of the kingdom of God. The message was, simply stated, that Jesus is the King. The apostolic burden was not just to get people into the church, but to see Jesus formed in His people and to see His name made a glory and a wonder in the earth. This is why the Great Commission was not just to make converts, but to **"make *disciples.*"** These true disciples were those who were taught to **"observe *all*"** that Jesus had commanded.

Day after day the apostles taught what they had been commanded. This was as much a fulfilling of the Great Commission as the preaching of the gospel for the salvation of souls. Seeing so many being born again was wonderful, but when we are born we are just beginning our life. The same is true when we are born again, again; this is just the beginning of our journey, not the end. The ultimate goal of the apostles was to see those who joined themselves to the Lord and become like Him. Anything less than this is a dilution of the gospel message.

We can never fulfill the Great Commission by just proclaiming Jesus as Savior; He must be Lord of all or He is not Lord at all. If there is just one word which could sum up the essence of the Great Commission, it is the word *all.* Jesus had been given *all* authority in heaven and on earth (see Matthew 28:18). True disciples were taught to **"observe *all*"** that He had commanded them. This message was *all*-encompassing to those who embraced it. Their faith was not just an appendage added to their lives, which required them to go to some meetings. Knowing Jesus, following Him day by day, in every place and situation, was fundamental to the life of the early church. He became *all* to them.

Jesus is the Way, the Truth, and the Life. We cannot truly know the Way and the Truth until He becomes our Life. The Way does not just believe a few fundamental truths about the Lord—the Way *is* the Lord. The Truth is not found by just agreeing with certain doctrines, even all Christian doctrines—the Truth is a Person who must be our whole life.

## WE MUST EAT THE WHOLE THING

Jesus was the Passover Lamb of God. When the children of Israel were instructed to partake of the first Passover lamb so that the angel of death would pass over them, they were instructed to eat the whole lamb, including its head and entrails, not leaving any of it over until morning (see Exodus 12:7-10). This was a prophetic statement that if we are going to partake of the Passover Lamb of God, we cannot pick and choose which parts of Him we want.

If we are going to partake of God's provision for us in His Son, we cannot say that we want His salvation but not His Lordship, nor His Holy Spirit, or the ministries He gave to the church so she might "**grow up in *all* aspects into Him**" (Ephesians 4:15). Until we are like Christ and do the works that He did, we have not been completed yet.

Paul wrote to the Corinthians that "**...the testimony concerning Christ was confirmed in you, so that you are not lacking in *any* gift... (I Corinthians 1:6-7).** All of the ministries and gifts of the Spirit are but aspects of Christ that He demonstrated when He walked the earth in the flesh. They are demonstrated in the church because He still dwells among us by the Holy Spirit. The functioning of any ministry is actually the moving of Christ within our midst. If we limit any of the gifts or ministries, we are rejecting that aspect of Christ. If we are going to be *all* we have been called to be, we must open our hearts to *all* of Him.

Therefore, the Great Commission cannot be fulfilled until all of the equipping ministries are working together. It may begin with an evangelist proclaiming the good news of salvation, but it must be followed up with the work of the apostles, prophets, pastors, and teachers. Philip is the only example in Scripture of one who was a pure evangelist (see Acts 8:4-8). But we see Philip needed others (Peter and John) to come and follow up his ministry so that the converts were established in the Lord. The foundation was not laid until they were made disciples, not just converts.

In the New Testament narrative of the formation of the church, we see that those who were converted were added to the church. Today it is estimated by some of our greatest evangelists that only about 5 percent of those who "make decisions for Christ" are added to the church. We should be thankful for any who are, but can we really call this the fulfilling of the Great Commission? What has caused this slide from all who confess Him, and then join the church, to just one out of every twenty? Can those who are not really joined to the church even be called "converts" if we are going to comply with the biblical definition of that word?

## HOW DO WE TEACH DISCIPLES TO OBSERVE ALL?

The apostle Paul gave a very clear outline for how disciples were to be taught to **"observe all"** that the Lord had commanded:

**And He gave some as apostles, and some as prophets, and some as evangelists, and some as pastors and teachers,**

**for the equipping of the saints for the work of service, to the building up of the body of Christ;**

**until we all attain to the unity of the faith, and of the knowledge of the Son of God, to a mature man, to the measure of the stature which belongs to the fulness of Christ.**

**As a result, we are no longer to be children, tossed here and there by waves, and carried about by every wind of doctrine, by the trickery of men, by craftiness in deceitful scheming;**

**but speaking the truth in love, we are to grow up in all aspects into Him, who is the head, even Christ,**

**from whom the whole body, being fitted and held together by that which every joint supplies, according to the proper working of each individual part, causes the growth of the body for the building up of itself in love (Ephesians 4:11-16).**

Here we see that no one man could perform the ministry required for the church to be equipped. Jesus was the Apostle, Prophet, Evangelist, Pastor, and Teacher. When He ascended He gave aspects of His ministry to many different ones. Together these five equipping ministries formed His complete ministry required to equip the disciples and cause them **"to grow up in *all* aspects into Him."** It is therefore apparent that the church will never become all that it is called to be until all of these ministries are functioning together.

It is also obvious according to this Scripture that if the church has not attained this stature, all of these ministries are still needed. They were clearly given *"**until** we attain* **to: 1) the unity of the faith, 2) the knowledge of the Son of God,** 3) **to a mature man,** 4) **the measure of the stature which belongs to the fulness of Christ."** Is there a church anywhere in the world which can rightfully claim this? If not, then we still need all of these ministries functioning in their place.

A main factor which constantly diverts the church and keeps her from being all she has been called to be, has been our tendency just to take whatever parts of the gospel we wanted and either reject or overlook the rest. We can never fulfill the Great Commission until we make disciples, not just converts, and teach them to observe *all* that the Lord has commanded us.

## THE POWER OF WEAKNESS

What was the gospel message preached by the first century church? How was it presented? How does it compare to what is generally presented as the gospel today? The apostle Paul gave the following explanation of the message he preached:

> **And when I came to you, brethren, I did not come with superiority of speech or of wisdom, proclaiming to you the testimony of God.**
>
> **For I determined to know nothing among you except Jesus Christ, and Him crucified.**
>
> **And I was with you in weakness and in fear and in much trembling.**

**And my message and my preaching were not in persuasive words of wisdom, but in demonstration of the Spirit and of power,**

**that your faith should not rest on the wisdom of men, but on the power of God (I Corinthians 2:1-5).**

**For the kingdom of God does not consist in words, but in power (I Corinthians 4:20).**

How does our preaching compare? Could it not be said that we try to come with boldness and confidence in our own persuasive words and methods more than in demonstration of the Spirit and power? Maybe this is the main reason our results tend to be so paltry in comparison.

This is probably why the Lord sent Peter to the Jews and Paul to the Gentiles. It really seems that the Lord got these backwards, at least to our natural way of thinking. Of course Paul could relate to the Jews much better than Peter could, since Peter was an ignorant fisherman. And Peter would be much more at home with the Gentiles and they with him. But the Lord put them both in a situation where they would be profoundly uncomfortable. It is easy to see why Paul came to the Gentiles **"in weakness and in fear and in much trembling."**

As Paul said to the Galatians, he knew his flesh was a trial to them (see Galatians 4:14). Both Peter and Paul were sent to preach to those who would be repelled by them in the flesh. The only way they could fulfill their commission was to be completely dependent on the Holy Spirit. When Peter did try to go to the Gentiles, he got into serious trouble at Antioch (see Galatians 2:11-14). When Paul insisted on going to the Jews, even though he was repeatedly warned by the Holy Spirit of what awaited him, he got into trouble (see Acts 21:27-30).

We also think that we are called to the ones for which we have the greatest burden. Paul unquestionably had a much greater burden for the Jews. He declared that he would give up his own salvation if it would lead to their salvation. Even so, Paul was not called to the Jews. Neither are we necessarily called to those whom we may have the greatest burden to see reached.

Paul's burden for the Jews was obviously a natural one. According to the flesh he was the "Hebrew of Hebrews." What did Paul himself write about this very factor?

> **For the mind set on the flesh is death, but the mind set on the Spirit is life and peace,**
>
> **because the mind set on the flesh is hostile toward God; for it does not subject itself to the law of God, for it is not even able to do so;**
>
> **and those who are in the flesh cannot please God (Romans 8:6-8).**
>
> **So then, brethren, we are under obligation, not to the flesh, to live according to the flesh—**
>
> **for if you are living according to the flesh, you must die** [or could we say, "have dead works"]; **but if by the Spirit you are putting to death the deeds of the body, you will live.**
>
> **For all who are being led by the Spirit of God, these are sons of God (Romans 8:12-14).**

A primary factor that keeps many of us from fulfilling our calling is the tendency to try and minister to those with whom we feel the most comfortable or to those whom we are the most like in our flesh. This basic compromise will be an easy bridge we can cross to start compromising the gospel.

## ARE WE TRUE DISCIPLES?

That leads us to another important question. Even when we make converts into disciples, are we making them into true disciples? Are our converts being converted by the cross or by our methodology? Are they really being led to Jesus, or to our denominations, our doctrines, or even just to us?

There has been a subtle, but profound perversion of the gospel in modern times. The message has been changed from Jesus having come to save us from our sins, to Him having come to save us from our troubles. This is not to imply that the Lord does not help us with our troubles, but when that is the foundation upon which someone is converted to the Lord, it is a very shallow one indeed. It is this perversion that keeps many from even sharing the good news until they see someone in a certain state of desperation. We need to be in desperation to come to the Lord, not because of our problems, but because of the conviction of sin.

Only the Holy Spirit can make a true disciple. He does it by bringing the conviction of sin that casts one in desperation upon the cross to find relief. If our conversion does not begin from desperation because of our sins, which causes us to cling to the cross for forgiveness, then we have started on the wrong foundation. There is a resurrection after the cross, but one cannot be resurrected until he has first died. Trying to impart the hope and benefits of the resurrection, without dying to our self-life on the cross, is a terrible and tragic delusion. Multitudes have been made to feel better about themselves, but in a condition that their eternal life is still in jeopardy.

Jesus is not coming "cap in hand" begging men to "accept Him." He still calls men the way He called them when He walked this earth.

**And He was saying to them all, "If anyone wishes to come after Me, let him deny himself, and take up his cross daily, and follow Me (Luke 9:23).**

**So therefore, no one of you can be My disciple who does not give up all of his own possessions (Luke 14:33).**

**For the love of Christ controls us, having concluded this, that one died for all, therefore all died;**

**and He died for all, that they who live should no longer live for themselves, but for Him who died and rose again on their behalf (II Corinthians 5:14-15).**

**Not everyone who says to Me, "Lord, Lord" will enter the kingdom of heaven; but he who does the will of My Father who is in heaven.**

**Many will say to Me on that day, "Lord, Lord" did we not prophesy in Your name, and in Your name cast out demons, and in Your name perform many miracles?"**

**And then I will declare to them, "I never knew you; depart from Me, you who practice lawlessness" (Matthew 7:21-23).**

When Jesus called His disciples it was for total commitment—they had to be willing to leave everything to follow Him. So do we. Nothing less than this is true discipleship. When we modify the message of the cross in order to make it acceptable, we destroy the power of that message to truly save. That is why Paul said, **"For Christ did not send me to baptize, but to preach the gospel, not in cleverness of speech, that the cross of Christ should not be made void. For the word of the cross is to those who are perishing**

**foolishness, but to us who are being saved it is the power of God (I Corinthians 1:17-18).** Adding our own cleverness to the message of the cross in order to make it palatable to men can compromise its very power to save.

## SUMMARY

True evangelism is not founded on a love for the lost as much as on a love for the Savior. It is not a man-centered message but rather Christ-centered. When Jesus is lifted up, not our churches, not our doctrines, but Jesus, then all men will be drawn. To lift Him up we must keep our attention upon Him. We cannot even let our love and concern for the lost eclipse our devotion to Him or it will lead to a perversion of the gospel.

True Christianity requires being born again by God's Spirit. This rebirth *initiates* the restoration of our union with Him, but it is the beginning. True Christianity is a journey to intimate fellowship with our Father through Jesus Christ. It was our fellowship with the Lord that was the most tragic loss of the Fall. If there is any way that true spiritual maturity can be measured—if there is any way we can determine the degree to which true redemption has worked in our lives, it will be by how close we have become to Him.

As we draw close to Him, becoming His disciples, we begin to behold His glory which changes us. Again, let us consider what is said in II Corinthians 3:18: **"But we all, with an unveiled face beholding as in a mirror the glory of the Lord, are being transformed into the same image from glory to glory, just as from the Lord, the Spirit."** Here we see that it is not just seeing the glory that we need, but seeing His glory **"with an unveiled face."** The veil is the flesh. When we are born again, we begin to see the kingdom of God because we are spiritually circumcised. The flesh must be cut away so we can see Him. Even so, *we do not change so we can fellowship with Him, but we are changed by our fellowship with Him.*

As the historian Will Durant observed, "Ceasar sought to change men by changing institutions. Jesus changed institutions by changing men." The gospel is not about building an institution, but building men. When the true wine of the true gospel is preached, it will burst out of the institutions that men build like new wine will burst out of an old wineskin. The true gospel is a life too powerful to be contained in our pitiful little structures.

This does not mean that the church should not have structure and order, but it must be one which is utterly flexible if it is to contain the true wine of the Spirit. We must let the life produce the structure, not the other way around. The early church had community and met from house to house *because* they had life, not in order to get it. They became the force that they were because the church was not the pattern for their church life—Jesus was the pattern. They were not following a formula or a form, but a Person.

It still seems that before the Spirit can move again in a great way, He must find those who are still **"formless and void" (Genesis 1:2)**. Those who think they have the answers, who think that they know how to build things in such a way that He will come, are almost always left behind. Then the Lord has to start His new moves with those who are basically full of fear and trembling, helpless and humble, but who do know and love the anointing, and who are willing to follow Him.

**He again fixes a certain day, "Today,"..."Today if you hear His voice, do not harden your hearts" (Hebrews 4:7).**

Thus says the Lord, "Heaven is My throne, and the earth is My footstool. Where then is a house you could build for Me? And where is a place that I may rest?

For My hand made all these things, thus all these things came into being," declares the Lord. "But to this one will I look [to be His dwelling place] to him who is humble and contrite of spirit and who trembles at My word" (Isaiah 66:1-2).

CHAPTER FIVE

# THE FOUNDATION OF APOSTLES

**So then you are no longer strangers and aliens, but you are fellow citizens with the saints, and are of God's household,**

**having been built upon the foundation of the apostles and prophets, Christ Jesus Himself being the corner stone**

**in whom the whole building, being fitted together is growing into a holy temple in the Lord;**

**in whom you also are being built together into a dwelling of God in the Spirit (Ephesians 2:19-22).**

IN THE LAST CHAPTER WE DISCUSSED HOW ALL of the gifts and ministries given to the church were aspects of the Lord's own ministry that were distributed to the church after His ascension. When all of the gifts and ministries are functioning in union with Him, He can be fully revealed through the church. In this chapter we will begin to study the structure of first century church life and its government, which was basically formed by the functioning of the gifts and ministries of the Spirit, established on the foundation laid by the apostles and prophets.

## THE APOSTOLIC MINISTRY

As we have stated often, the first and most important thing lost by the fall of man was his intimate relationship to God. The whole plan of redemption that was added after the Fall, was designed to restore the intimate relationship between men and their God. If there is any way we can measure the degree to which redemption has worked in our lives, or that we have spiritually matured, it would be by our intimacy with God. God created man for fellowship and His ultimate goal is to have His habitation among men. TO BE A DWELLING PLACE OF GOD IS THE ULTIMATE CALLING OF MEN. The apostolic ministry is given to the church as a master builder to help build the habitation of God.

Redemption is but the first step in restoring man's former state of fellowship with the Lord. However, the Lord's plan of redemption is much more than just restoring us to the former state before the Fall. As we are born again, we become a part of the *"new creation,"* (see Galatians 6:15) which greatly transcends the original creation. Now we do not just have fellowship with God, but we are being made into His dwelling place. To be born is just the first step of life. To be born again is but the first step of our spiritual life. It is the beginning, not the end. Evangelists are concerned with the beginning; apostles are devoted to the final result, the full maturity of the church.

God does not just fellowship with the new creation; He has come to live in us. This is much higher than what Adam, Moses, or even the disciples experienced before the Holy Spirit was given. This is why the Lord said to the disciples that it was better for them that He go away, so that the Holy Spirit would come. It was truly the most glorious and awesome time for mankind to have the Creator walking *among* men. Even so, it is even more awesome to have Him living *in* us!

This is not to belittle redemption, which is essential before we can even return to fellowship with God, much less become His dwelling place. Even so, we must recognize that redemption is not the ultimate goal, but rather the initial step. Redemption gets us back to "ground zero," the place from which man fell. We are called to go on from there to much greater heights.

True Christianity is more than just acknowledging certain truths, or even living by them. True Christianity is becoming a **"new creation,"** that is in even higher unity with our Creator than the first creation. God is in us! He did not just come to change our thinking or just change our behavior; He came to live in us.

The apostolic ministry is especially devoted to seeing the church become the temple of the Lord. Therefore, if there is any way to measure the overall fruitfulness of an apostolic ministry it would be by the manifest presence of the Lord in His church. Is the church abiding in Him so that He can manifest Himself through us? We must always keep in mind that we do not change so we can fellowship with God, but we are changed by our fellowship with Him. That fellowship was made possible by the cross. Regardless of how mature we become, we can never enter the Lord's presence by our own merit, but only through the blood.

## THE LAST GREAT MOVEMENT OF THE CHURCH AGE?

Before the end of this age comes, there will be a movement that will bring true apostolic Christianity to the church.

This can only be done by a restored apostolic ministry. The ministry that opened the church age will be the one that closes it. The Spirit is now moving relentlessly toward that which will again be truly apostolic. This is our quest—to see true, apostolic Christianity restored to the earth. This is not just so the church can become what we are called to be, even though that is important. The church must become what she is called to be for a much higher purpose so that the Lord can dwell among us.

What does this mean? First, it means that Jesus will be in us to do the works He did when He walked the earth. Second, it will mean that the church will accurately represent Him to the world. Our words must become His words, and our works His works.

As we read from Ephesians 4 in the previous chapter, when all of the ministries are fully restored and functioning in the church, believers will be:

1) adequately equipped for the ministry,

2) come **"to the unity of the faith"** (which is much more than just a unity around doctrine),

3) come to **" the full knowledge of the Son of God,"**

4) be raised **"to a mature man to the measure of the stature** which belongs to the fulness of Christ,"

5) **"no longer be children"** (or immature),

6) no longer be tossed about the waves, the winds of doctrine, and the trickery of men, and

7) **"grow up in *all aspects* into"** the Head.

This is the apostolic commission, and it is far beyond human genius or ability. If we are going to be apostolic, our labor will not be finished until Christ is formed in His people. We must not let any other emphasis eclipse this basic work. We are looking for far more than the manifestation of the sons of God; we are looking for the manifestation of the Son of God in His people. Jesus must always be the focus of our ministry if we are ever to be truly apostolic.

The ministry of the apostle is to bear the travail of spiritual labor until Christ is formed *in* the church, not that the church would come into any certain form (see Galatians 4:19). The apostles to the early church did certain things to achieve and maintain order in the congregations, but they did not emphasize any specific form except the forming of Christ within. The Lord's emphasis and the apostolic emphasis was devoted to changing the heart, not just the institution. When hearts are changed, institutions either give way to the Spirit, or burst like old wineskins.

Changing externals such as where and how we meet cannot by itself impart life. As discussed, the early church had community and met from house to house *because* they had life, not in order to get it. Again, the church is not the pattern for the church; Jesus is the pattern for the church. The church does have order and form, but when form becomes the primary emphasis, there is almost always a fall from the grace that can only come from abiding in the Lord Himself.

## WHAT IS AN APOSTLE?

The following are some of the more prominent characteristics of an apostle that we can derive from the New Testament:

1) *Apostles are spiritual fathers*. Paul said that we have many teachers but not many fathers (see I Corinthians 4:15). The same is true in the church today. There are many outstanding teachers and preachers, but not many fathers. Many are called spiritual fathers because of their age, just as most men become physical fathers when they are young. However, being a spiritual father has little to do with age. A spiritual father reproduces his ministry in others. Very few in ministry actually seem to do this.

Even so, just the ability to reproduce our ministry in others does not make us an apostle. All of the equipping ministries are supposed to do this. To be apostolic is more than reproducing our ministry in others, it is seeing Christ formed in the whole church.

2) *Apostles establish churches*. This was an obvious result of apostolic ministry in the first century. However, there is a big difference between establishing churches and building franchises. The churches in the first century were so unique that each one listed in Revelation needed a different word from the Lord, even though they all existed in the same general region at the same time. Our God is the blessed Creator who makes every snowflake different. Possibly the single, most tragic way that we have misrepresented God is by our boring uniformity. Every congregation, every person, every meeting, should be gloriously

unique and interesting if we are to reflect our blessed Creator.

The Lord is the only One who can build His church. He does this through apostles, who He uses as "wise master builders." Even so, the Lord will be both the Designer and Builder of His own house. If we are going to be a part of a truly apostolic church, we must question whether we are building that which the Lord wants to dwell, or are we just building that which will attract people? If our true motivation is to attract people, we will not build that which will bring the manifest presence of the Lord. If we build that which the Lord truly inhabits, we may or may not attract many people to it, but that is not our concern.

The Lord does care about numbers. He desires for all men to be saved. Even so, there are places where the conditions are such that His presence may not draw many people, and there are places where He will draw far more than a human organization could contain. We are not here to be big or small, but to do His will, to abide in Him so that He can abide in us.

We must also consider that just building churches will not make one an apostle. Evangelists, pastors, teachers, or prophets may all be used to establish churches, as well as those who are not recognized as being one of the equipping ministries. The first century church at Antioch was not birthed by apostles, but it gave birth to new apostolic ministries. It is likely that if the apostolic team from Jerusalem had birthed this church, it may not have been able to give birth to the new type of missionary apostle who came forth from her. Only a new wineskin can hold God's new wine. However, the Lord is also going to serve aged, refined wine at His banquet, which He is preparing for all people (see Isaiah 25:6). We should have a taste for both!

3) *Apostles impart God's government.* We cannot have a complete revelation of who Jesus is without understanding that He is the **"King of kings" (I Timothy 6:15).** Jesus is the ultimate representative of God's authority, and if we are becoming like Him we will both walk in and help to establish His authority in the earth.

The Lord made it clear that His authority was not like the Gentiles or present human authority. His authority was based on love and service. The most devastating mistakes in church history have been the result of church leaders imposing church government that was in the form of human authority rather than that of the kingdom. Earthly authority is in contrast to the very nature and Spirit of the Lord, which will not produce righteousness in the people.

The Lord's own leadership style is also in striking contrast to that of most churches and movements throughout history, which deserves a considerable amount of attention in our study. The Lord did not impart a system of government, but built men who had the law in their hearts. Even if we have the best system of government, it will be bad government if we do not have good people in it. Likewise, even bad systems of government can be good government with good people in them.

The government of God is not just a system or organization, but an anointing. We only have true spiritual authority to the degree that the King lives within us. When men derive their authority from a position in a system, they can maintain influence long after the anointing has departed from them. This alone has caused repeated tragedies in church history.

We must also recognize that lawlessness is one of the greatest enemies at the end of the age. Though it is likely that the truth of God's government has yet to be discovered by the modern church, it will not be built upon the rebellion of tearing down what now exists. Even earthly governments that are in contrast to His nature are ordained by Him for keeping order until His kingdom comes. Let us not confuse the fact that even though His authority is based on love and service, it still contains discipline and judgment.

4) *An apostle has seen the Lord*. This is one of the criteria which Paul stated as proof of apostolic

authority when defending his own ministry (see I Corinthians 9:1). Obviously this means that an apostle must literally see the Lord—a prerequisite for an apostolic commission. This is because Jesus is the pattern of the house that the apostle is commissioned to build. Moses, who built the first dwelling place of God on the earth, had to go up on the mountain and see the pattern of that dwelling place before he could build it. Likewise, the apostle, who is called to labor until Christ is formed, must see the glory of who He now is, and have this branded on his heart and mind.

When we are captured by the glory of who He is, we will not be prone to be distracted by the ways which may seem good, but are still according to the flesh. Devotion to patterns and formulas is a basic symptom of witchcraft. Witchcraft is the counterfeit of true spiritual authority. If we are to be delivered from the tendency to use human devices in trying to accomplish the purposes of God, we must see Him on His throne in such a way that it is much more than a doctrine to us. Having literally, visibly seen the resurrected Christ is required of true apostolic ministry.

5) *The apostle is a witness of His resurrection.* This is related to the last point, which is to have seen Him in His resurrection glory, but it also speaks of proclaiming His resurrection. It is by seeing the glory of His resurrection that our proclamation is empowered.

In Acts 1:22 we see that the office of the apostle was given to be a witness of His resurrection. In Acts 4:33 we see that power was given to the church to be a witness of His resurrection. In Romans 1:4 we see that Jesus **"was declared the Son of God with power by the resurrection from the dead."**

The resurrection was the central theme of the gospel preached by the first century apostles. Yet, having studied the writings and messages of the great voices in church history, it is hard to find more than a cursory address on this most foundational truth by any of them since the first century. I have listened to thousands of sermons, many by some of the greatest preachers of our time, and I do not recall a single in-depth message being given on this subject unless it was an obligatory Easter sermon. Could the neglect of this most basic truth be a primary reason why the church today is so far from the apostolic pattern and power of the first century church? It certainly has much to do with it.

Charles Spurgeon went so far as to say, "There are very few *Christians* who believe in the resurrection." When I first read this I thought it was a misprint, but then the Holy Spirit witnessed to me that it was true. True faith is more than just an intellectual assent to certain facts. It is by believing in our *hearts*, not our minds, that will result in righteousness (see Romans 10:10). We can believe in the doctrine of the resurrection without really believing it in our hearts. If we really believed in our hearts, most of our lives would be radically different than they are now. We would not be as consumed with the tyranny of the temporary and would be given fully to the things that are eternal. What Spurgeon was implying was that we give intellectual assent to the fact of the *resurrection,* but go on living our lives as if it did not exist. As Paul wrote in I Corinthians 15:13-14, if we do not believe in the resurrection, our faith is in vain.

## APOSTOLIC VISION

Moses was a man of vision. He actually saw the Tabernacle in detail on the Mount before he was able to begin its construction (see Exodus 25:40). A true spiritual vision is not just something we decide to come up with; *a true spiritual vision must originate from God.*

The prophet Haggai said that **"the latter glory of this house will be greater than the former..." (Haggai 2:9).** He did not say that the house was greater, but that the glory in it would be greater. The apostolic goal is not focused on the house as much as on the glory of the One who is to inhabit the house. True apostolic vision is Christ-centered, not church-centered. The apostolic call is to lead men to Christ, not just to church. If men are truly led to Christ they will end up in church, but the reverse is not necessarily true. Many are drawn to the church for various reasons, but never come to know the Lord. What good is the most glorious temple if the Lord is not in it? If He is in it, the temple will not be what gets your attention. The great apostolic prayer was:

**I pray that the eyes of your heart may be enlightened, so that you may know what is the hope of His calling, what are the riches of the glory of His inheritance in the saints,**

**and what is the surpassing greatness of His power toward us who believe. These are in accordance with the working of the strength of His might (Ephesians 1:18-19).**

It does not say we should come to know what is the hope of *our* calling or *our* inheritance. Neither will anything of true eternal value ever be accomplished by *our* power. One of the most subtle, but devastating deceptions that we can fall into is the over-emphasis of who we are in Christ in place of who He is in us. We do need to know who we are and what our calling is, but we must never allow that to eclipse our devotion to seeing Him.

## APOSTOLIC CHARACTER

Apostles are called to be God's master-builders of His dwelling place, the church. We can see aspects of the character required for this task in the lives of all who were used to build His dwelling places in Scripture. Of Moses, the first to build a dwelling place for God, it was said:

**By faith Moses, when he was come to years, refused to be called the son of Pharaoh's daughter;**

**choosing rather to suffer affliction with the people of God, that to enjoy the pleasures of sin for a season;**

> **esteeming the reproach of Christ greater riches than the treasures in Egypt; for he had respect unto the** [spiritual] **recompense of the reward (Hebrews 11:24-26 KJV).**

Here we see that Moses chose to sacrifice the greatest of worldly opportunities to serve the purposes of God, refusing to be **"called the son of Pharaoh's daughter."** The apostle Paul, as the archetype of the biblical apostle, did the same, refusing the high position of influence he could have attained as the Pharisee of Pharisees.

Moses chose to **"suffer affliction with the people of God,"** esteeming the sufferings of Christ as **"greater riches"** than all of the treasures of Egypt. Paul also walked in continual persecution, dangers, and setbacks, viewing all of them as making greater opportunities for the gospel, and even a basis for his authority. As a Roman citizen, Paul was obviously in a high position as a member of the aristocracy of the world's greatest empire, yet by his own admission he counted every such title and privilege "as dung" (see Philippians 3:8). Just as the earth does not even register as much more than a speck of dust in the great expanse of God's universe, all of the riches of this earth could not be compared to a speck of dust in the eternal dwelling place of God. To suffer any kind of persecution for the sake of His gospel is a treasure far beyond any earthly wealth.

Moses rejected the temporary pleasures of sin. All of the apostles walked in a life above reproach, sanctified and holy to the Lord. They were examples to the church, but they did not do this just to be examples. They dwelt in the presence of a holy God. When we view the beauty of His holiness, we will hate even the garment tainted by sin. God is holy, and we cannot really love Him without loving purity. Just as Moses *chose* to suffer affliction for the purposes of God, we too have a choice as to whether we sin or not. If we are to be an apostolic church, we must begin to choose to walk uprightly before the Lord.

Moses' vision was on the (spiritual) recompense of the reward. It is often said that some people are so heavenly minded that they are not any earthly good. Those about whom this is said may be close to being apostolic. What men who ever walked the earth after Jesus were more heavenly minded than the apostles? An overwhelming problem in the ministry today is that most are too earthly minded to be any spiritual good. "**... For he** (Moses) **endured, as *seeing him who is invisible*" (Hebrews 11:27 KJV)**. Spiritual vision requires that what we see with the eyes of our hearts is more real to us than what we see with our natural eyes. *We must see that which is invisible to others.*

## SUMMARY

The apostolic ministry will be restored to the church before the end comes. The apostolic message is not in word only, but in demonstration of the Spirit and power. This demonstration will be a church that fully reveals the nature and power of her Lord. We cannot settle for cheap substitutes. Like the restoration of every other ministry to the church, there will be many pretenders before the real appears. However, we can know for certain by the sure testimony of Scripture that the real is coming.

The apostolic ministry requires a commission from God and it requires the substance of spiritual authority. True apostles will not come with theories, forms, recipes, and formulas, but with an impartation of the true life and power of the Lord. This is nothing less than to be the temple of God, to dwell in His presence, and to manifest the sweet aroma of the knowledge of Him in every place. Before the end, such an apostolic church will turn the world upside down again or turn an upside down world right side up.

The Lord praised the church at Ephesus because they **"put to the test those who call themselves apostles, and they are not..." (Revelation 2:2).** We cannot allow our spiritual currency to be devalued by calling those apostles who do not qualify. Even so, just as we must receive a prophet **"in the name of a prophet" (Matthew 10:41)** to receive a prophet's reward, the same is true of every ministry. If we receive an apostle as just a teacher, we will not get the full reward of having received an apostle, all that we will get is teaching. It is right that we put to the test those who call themselves apostles, and reject those who are not, but let us also be looking expectantly for those who really are and receive them properly.

# CHAPTER SIX

# APOSTOLIC TRAVAIL

O BVIOUSLY, FOR THERE TO BE A TRULY APOSTOLIC church, there must be an apostolic ministry restored to the church. The ministry that opened the church age will be the one that closes it. As we previously read in Ephesians 4:13, this ministry was given to the church **"until we all attain to the unity of the faith, and of the knowledge of the Son of God, to a mature man, to the measure of the stature which belongs to the fulness of Christ."** As it is quite apparent that no church has yet attained to this stature, much less **"all,"** then this ministry is still needed for the equipping of the saints for their purpose. This is now being understood across a broad spectrum of the body of Christ.

Because the need for the apostolic ministry is understood by much of the church, this can lead us to accept a cheap substitute for the authentic ministry. There are now many who call themselves apostles. They may be good evangelists, great teachers, mighty in the Scriptures with depth of insight into the Lord's purposes, but this does not make them apostles. Many have proven prophetic gifts and are very effective mobilizers and organizers, but all of these together still does not make one an apostle.

The church is first a family, not an organization. However, much of what we think of as the church today is really founded on organization, not relationship. Likewise, much of what is now believed to be apostolic is founded on organization first and then on relationships which are based on devotion to the organization. If we are going to be truly apostolic, this must be reversed. This is why we see in the Scriptures that the essence of the first century apostolic ministry was to travail, to birth, and not just to organize. For there to be an apostolic ministry, there must be apostolic travail.

In Galatians 4:19 Paul writes, **"My children, with whom I am again in labor until Christ is formed in you."** The apostolic travail Paul endured so that Christ would be formed in the church literally translated means "to be in pain." When the Lord called Paul He said, **"I will show him how much he must suffer for My name's sake"** (Acts 9:16). Later he was to write, **"For just as the sufferings of Christ are ours in abundance, so also our comfort is abundant through Christ (II Corinthians 1:5).**

The true apostolic ministry still requires sufferings in abundance. True Christianity is a life of sacrifice. It requires that in everything we live for the Lord and others, not ourselves. As Paul also wrote:

> **But we have this treasure in earthen vessels, that the surpassing greatness of the power may be of God and not from ourselves;**
>
> **we are afflicted in every way, but not crushed; perplexed, but not despairing;**
>
> **persecuted, but not forsaken; struck down, but not destroyed;**
>
> **always carrying about in the body the dying of Jesus, that the life of Jesus also may me manifested in our body.**

> **For we who live are constantly being delivered over to death for Jesus' sake, that the life of Jesus also may be manifested in our mortal flesh (II Corinthians 4:7-11).**

The apostles had the power to impart spiritual life to the degree that the dying of Jesus worked in them. Death is the path to life in Christ. If we will have true faith, there is no other path. When we see the travail, pain, and suffering that is fundamental to this ministry, there will probably not be as many claiming to be apostles. Because of the popular doctrines that have attempted to remove suffering from the faith this is incomprehensible to many Western Christians today. But it is still the essence of true faith and will be a foundation of true, apostolic ministry. This is why when Paul's apostolic ministry was challenged, he responded by recounting his sufferings for the sake of the gospel.

This understanding must be recovered if we are going to have true apostolic ministry restored. For this purpose let us continue reviewing what both the Lord and the first century apostles said about this crucial subject of self-denial and suffering for the sake of righteousness.

> **Then Jesus said to His disciples, "If anyone wishes to come after Me, let him deny himself, and take up his cross, and follow Me.**
>
> **For whoever wishes to save his life shall lose it; but whoever loses his life for My sake shall find it (Matthew 16:24-25).**

To deny oneself is almost unheard of in the world. It is an increasingly foreign mentality to modern life, but if we are going to be true followers of Christ, it must be our nature. As Paul explained:

**In no way alarmed by your opponents—which is a sign of destruction for them, but of salvation for you, and that too, from God.**

**For to you is has been granted for Christ's sake, not only to believe in Him, but also to suffer for His sake (Philippians 1:28-29).**

This was addressed to all believers, not just apostles. The principles of sacrifice that we see attributed to biblical apostles were the same for all believers. However, the apostles as leaders had to first lay down their lives as a living sacrifice and, with but a couple of exceptions, they finished their course in martyrdom. As Paul wrote to the Romans:

**The Spirit Himself bears witness with our spirit that we are children of God,**

**and if children, heirs also, heirs of God and fellow heirs with Christ, if indeed we suffer with Him in order that we may also be glorified with Him (Romans 8:16-17).**

"If" is one of the biggest words in the Scripture. It implies an absolute condition. We are told here that we are heirs of God and fellow heirs with Christ "**if**" we suffer with Him. That is why Paul also wrote:

**That I may know Him, and the power of His resurrection and the fellowship of His sufferings, being conformed to His death;**

**in order that I may attain to the resurrection from the dead.**

**Not that I have already obtained it, or have already become perfect, but I press on in order that I may lay hold of that for which also I was laid hold of by Christ Jesus (Philippians 3:10-12).**

Amazingly, Paul wrote this near the end of his life. Having endured and accomplished so much, he was still pressing on, not feeling as though he had yet attained. Of course, this had nothing to do with his salvation which he attained the day he first believed in Christ. What he did not feel that he had yet attained was to the high calling of God in Christ. How often do we start feeling content after just a few accomplishments, and begin to rest more on what we have done, rather than pressing ahead until we have fully completed our course in victory? There was no thought of retirement with the apostles! As Peter stated it:

**Therefore, since Christ has suffered in the flesh, arm yourselves also with the same purpose, because he who has suffered in the flesh has ceased from sin,**

**so as to live the rest of the time in the flesh no longer for the lusts of men, but for the will of God (I Peter 4:1-2).**

Our time in this life is not for our happiness, **"but for the will of God."** There is no greater joy or peace that we can know in this life than that which comes from doing the will of God. However, if our own satisfaction is the purpose of our life, we will not find it here and we will also sacrifice the greatest of satisfactions for eternity, just as Paul wrote in I Corinthians 9:24-27:

**Do you not know that those who run a race all run, but only one receives a prize? Run in such a way that you may win.**

**And everyone who competes in the games exercises self-control in all things. They then**

do it to receive a perishable wreath, but we an imperishable.

Therefore I run in such a way, as not without aim; I box in such a way, as not beating the air;

but I buffet my body and make it my slave, lest possibly, after I have preached to others, I myself should be disqualified.

This text reveals the spiritual principle that to the degree we live by the law of sacrifice of the flesh, we will receive and be able to give spiritual life. Again, this is not for our salvation or even our acceptance with God, which is gained only through the cross of Jesus. However, it is by being united with Him in His death that life is released through us just as it was through Him.

For the mind set on the flesh is death, but the mind set on the Spirit is life and peace...

for if you are living according to the flesh, you must die; but if by the Spirit you are putting to death the deeds of the body, you will live.

For all who are being led by the Spirit of God, these are sons of God.

For you have not received a spirit of slavery leading to fear again, but you have received a spirit of adoption as sons by which we cry out, "Abba! Father!"

The Spirit Himself bears witness with our spirit that we are children of God,

and if children, heirs also, heirs of God and fellow heirs with Christ, if indeed we suffer with Him in order that we may also be glorified with Him.

**For I consider that the sufferings of this present time are not worthy to be compared with the glory that is to be revealed to us.**

**For the anxious longing of the creation waits eagerly for the revealing of the sons of God (Romans 8:6, 13-19).**

Adam lived in a perfect world and yet chose to sin. The whole creation that was under his authority suffered because of his transgression. Since then the whole creation has been waiting for those who will live in the darkest of times and yet choose to obey, laying down their own lives and self-interests for the sake of those under their authority.

The kingdom of God is the domain of God. It is the return of His dominion to the earth that we are serving. The first Adam fell and gave his domain over to the evil one, who he had obeyed. As the **"last Adam,"** Jesus remained faithful in order to return the domain of Adam to the Father. We become joint heirs with Him over this domain as we prove our faithfulness by living for Him and not ourselves. This sacrifice is incomprehensible to the fallen human nature, but it is the path to true life and a life that will last forever.

Paul exhorted, **"through many tribulations we must enter the kingdom of God"** (Acts 14:22). This is a basic, spiritual principle that we enter the kingdom through tribulations. We all want to claim "kingdom living" but are we willing to go through the gate? This principle applies to us as individuals as well as the whole creation. The kingdom age is going to be ushered in through a great tribulation. We must therefore view tribulations as a blessing and not as a curse. They are a gate for entering into the full purpose of God.

**Consider it all joy, my brethren, when you encounter various trials,**

**knowing that the testing of your faith produces endurance.**

**And let endurance have its perfect result, that you may be perfect and complete, lacking in nothing (James 1:2-4).**

One of the most important lessons for every believer to learn is not to waste their trials. Every one of them is an opportunity to enter the kingdom. As Peter stated it:

**In this you greatly rejoice, even though now for a little while, if necessary, you have been distressed by various trials,**

**that the proof of your faith, being more precious than gold which is perishable, even though tested by fire, may be found to result in praise and glory and honor at the revelation of Jesus Christ; (I Peter 1:6-7).**

If we just esteemed the dealings of God even half as much as we tend to esteem earthly riches, the church would again be turning the world upside down with the power of the gospel. We would be very different people. When we learn to esteem sufferings according to their true value, we will again turn the world upside down. For this reason the Psalmist wrote: **"Precious in the sight of the Lord is the death of His godly ones"** (Psalm 116:15). The Lord esteems the death of His people because death is the path to true life in Christ. The Lord knows it is only when we are willing to lay down our lives that we will truly find them.

Before there can be a resurrection, there must be a death. Before we can walk in resurrection power, we must first die to ourselves. This is probably the one aspect of Christianity that has been the most avoided since the first century. It is certainly the main reason why the world has witnessed so little, true, apostolic Christianity since. We have allowed glib clichés such as: "They are so heavenly minded they are not any earthly good" to rob us of sound, biblical truth that reveals the true nature of our calling. The truth is that we have been so earthly minded that we have had little, true, spiritual power. Before the end comes, that will change. True, apostolic Christianity will be released on the earth again. When it has been recovered the kingdom will come and the whole creation will end its long travail for the return of her Creator.

The fall began when Satan began looking at his own, God imparted glory. When pride entered, he turned to his own way and carried with him all who were prone to live for themselves rather than their Creator. Jesus, who had much greater glory being the very Son of God, through even the greatest of trials, did not think of Himself but only of the Father's interests. Those who will be heirs with Him will be trusted with greater glory than Satan ever knew, as they, too, will be His sons and daughters. They, too, will have proven that they love the truth, and they love the Lord, more than they love their own lives.

Those who have been emptied of self-will and selfish ambition will be filled with His glory. Such will be the ones who are worthy to be the bride of the Lamb. This lifestyle which is so foreign to the self-preservation of the fallen world, puts the ax to the very root of the tree which has released all of the present evil into the world. It is therefore the most threatening and incomprehensible challenges to the present spirit of the world, and therefore the greatest witness of the kingdom of God.

So then, brethren, we are under obligation, not to the flesh, to live according to the flesh—

for if you are living according to the flesh, you must die; but if by the Spirit you are putting to death the deeds of the body, you will live.

For all who are being led by the Spirit of God, these are sons of God.

For you have not received a spirit of slavery leading to fear again, but you have received a spirit of adoption as sons by which we cry out, "Abba! Father!"

The Spirit Himself bears witness with our spirit that we are children of God,

and if children, heirs also, heirs of God and fellow heirs with Christ, if indeed we suffer with Him in order that we may also be glorified with Him.

For I consider that the sufferings of this present time are not worthy to be compared with the glory that is to be revealed to us.

For the anxious longing of the creation waits eagerly for the revealing of the sons of God.

For the creation was subjected to futility, not of its own will, but because of Him who subjected it, in hope

that the creation itself also will be set free from its slavery to corruption into the freedom of the glory of the children of God.

For we know that the whole creation groans and suffers the pains of childbirth together until now.

**And not only this, but also we ourselves, having the first fruits of the Spirit, even we ourselves groan within ourselves, waiting eagerly for our adoption as sons, the redemption of our body (Romans 8:12-23).**

## SUMMARY

Again, I repeat—the foundation of the church is Jesus Christ. This is more than just the teaching about Him; as we see in the first century church, it is the Lord Himself moving in their midst. The history of the early church is essentially the recorded deeds of God moving among them. The church was not built on creeds or programs, but on a living relationship with Jesus Christ. They demonstrated His presence with them day by day. The church was not recognized just by the doctrines to which it held, but by the presence of the Lord in their midst. Such was the nature of the true church in the beginning, and such will be the nature of the true church at the end. In Acts 4:13-14, as Peter and John stood before the Sanhedrin, we see a good example of this:

**Now as they observed the confidence of Peter and John, and understood that they were uneducated and untrained men, they were marveling, and began to recognize them as having been with Jesus.**

**And seeing the man who had been healed standing with them, they had nothing to say in reply.**

Those who had **"been with Jesus"** were easily recognized. It is to the degree that we abide in Him, spend time with Him, and walk with Him that we will again be recognized as being true believers. When this happens, we, like the early apostles, will have evidence that He is in our midst because those who have been healed will stand with us.

In the early church it was obvious that the Lord might manifest Himself and do extraordinary works through any believer at any time, but He did have leaders. These leaders did not just have authority because they were appointed, but because the Lord was with them *to lead*. Peter boldly stepped out to preach the gospel on the Day of Pentecost, and then to the Gentiles at the home of Cornelius. Because he followed the Lord, he repeatedly lead the church in the new directions that the Lord wanted to go. The apostles were accustomed to performing great miracles and even raising the dead. Leadership was not just a position; it was an action verb! Such was the nature of the apostolic ministry that laid the foundation in the first century, and we can expect the apostolic authority which will be restored at the end to be like it.

It was also the nature of the apostolic leaders to recognize and support what the Lord did through any believer. When they heard that Samaria was receiving the word of the Lord through Phillip, they sent apostles to help lay a solid foundation in the believers there. When they heard that the Gentiles in Antioch had received the word, they sent Barnabas to help encourage and establish them. In this the leaders did not just lead, but followed the Holy Spirit and supported His ministry through whomever He chose to use.

However, the church was not recognized just by the apostles who ministered to it, but by the Lord Himself being among them. Like "the church in the wilderness," they followed the cloud by day and the pillar of fire by night. When He moved, so did they. When He stopped, they pitched their tents where He was. They only went where the presence of the Lord led them. They followed the Lamb, the living God—not just a formula. The temple of the Lord was built out of living stones. The church was recognized simply by the people He inhabited.

The first century church exhibited a boldness that sent shock waves throughout the world. This boldness cannot be explained by the mere agreement with teachings. This boldness came from the living reality of Jesus in the midst of His people. Teaching was important, and the accuracy of their doctrine was firmly established by the Scriptures. Even so, they were not those who had just heard about the Lord, but those who followed Him. Their boldness was the result of the living God being in their midst. They grew in the knowledge of Him, but even more than that, they grew closer to Him. He was the reality of their lives.

The ultimate purpose of the Lord for every believer is that they become like Him and do the works that He did. His people are to be His witnesses, not because they have seen and known Him but because He is with them, now. It was the presence of the Lord, present tense, that gave the first century church its dynamic authority to impact the world with the gospel and it will be the same for the apostolic church that will be raised up again before the end comes. This is our ultimate quest, to be a dwelling place for the Lord. This is the purpose of apostles and all of the other ministries given to the church—to make us into His habitation.

To really believe the testimony of Scripture is not just to believe that these things were done, but to live in the reality of them, now. To really believe the Scriptures is witnessed by doing what is written in them. Anything less is the delusion of a religious spirit that will give glory to what God has done in order to justify neglecting or even persecuting what He is now doing. When the real nature of apostolic Christianity is revealed again, it will expose every pretender. Like the early church, the last day apostolic church can expect the worst persecution to come from those who claim to be Christians, who will claim most vehemently to be the protectors of the truth. Good has always been the worst enemy of best. Those who have settled for a good thing will be the most offended when something better comes. This persecution helps to separate the wheat from the chaff.

Let us guard our hearts by humbling ourselves with the reality of just how far short we are of the biblical stature of the church. We must rise above building our own little ministries if we are to be a part of building the true church. To build the true church we must rise above preaching the church and preach the kingdom, which is the glorious person and domain of the King. It is His glory that we must seek, not our own, if we will again be apostolic.

# CHAPTER SEVEN

# JEWISH ROOTS AND GENTILE BRANCHES

W E MUST TAKE THE TIME TO CAREFULLY EXAMINE the first century church so we can better understand the foundation of the church. If the foundation is not right, whatever is built upon it will be off to that degree. If we are to see true, New Testament Christianity restored to the earth, we must recover the true foundation. Then we will be able to understand to what we are being restored. Before the end of this age, the church will again be the pure, chaste bride that the Lamb is worthy to have.

## THE SIGN

On the Day of Pentecost, the Spirit descended on the disciples and they received the gift of tongues. As the apostle Paul would later explain, this gift was given for **"a sign"** **(I Corinthians 14:22).** This sign that was given when the Spirit first came upon the church is very important for us to understand, a key to which is found in Genesis 11:1-9.

> **Now the whole earth used the same language and the same words.**

And it came about as they journeyed east, that they found a plain in the land of Shinar and settled there.

And they said to one another, "Come, let us make bricks and burn them thoroughly." And they used brick for stone, and they used tar for mortar.

And they said, "Come, let us build for ourselves a city, and a tower whose top will reach into heaven, and let us make for ourselves a name; lest we be scattered abroad over the face of the whole earth."

And the LORD came down to see the city and the tower which the sons of men had built.

And the LORD said, "Behold, they are one people, and they all have the same language. And this is what they began to do, and now nothing which they purpose to do will be impossible for them.

Come, let Us go down and there confuse their language, that they may not understand one another's speech."

So the LORD scattered them abroad from there over the face of the whole earth; and they stopped building the city.

Therefore its name was called Babel, because there the LORD confused the language of the whole earth; and from there the LORD scattered them abroad over the face of the whole earth.

In contrast to what happened at Babel, on the Day of Pentecost for the first time since that infamous tower, a gift was given so that men all understood in a common language, as we see in Acts 2:5-12:

Now there were Jews living in Jerusalem, devout men, from every nation under heaven.

And when this sound occurred, the multitude came together, and were bewildered, because they were each one hearing them speak in his own language.

And they were amazed and marveled, saying, "Why, are not all these who are speaking Galileans?

"And how is it that we each hear them in our own language to which we were born?

"Parthians and Medes and Elamites, and residents of Mesopotamia, Judea and Cappadocia, Pontus and Asia,

Phrygia and Pamphylia, Egypt and the districts of Libya around Cyrene, and visitors from Rome, both Jews and proselytes,

Cretans and Arabs—we hear them in our own tongues speaking of the mighty deeds of God."

And they all continued in amazement and great perplexity, saying to one another, "What does this mean?"

This sign was a powerful statement that the church was to be the antithesis to the Tower of Babel where men's languages were scattered. Men from every nation and tongue would be gathered by the church to speak the only language that could ever, truly unite men again—the message of the glory of God, who is Jesus Christ. He is the Word of God, the Communication from God, through Whom eventually all will be gathered together.

Since that time we can look at history and say that the gospel has seemingly done more scattering than gathering.

However, the Word of God is forever settled. It will come to pass that when Jesus is truly lifted up, not the church, not our doctrines, nor our personalities, all men will be drawn to Him. Jesus is the desire of every human heart. Before the end of this age the church will see Jesus as He is, and present Him as He is, and multitudes from every nation will come.

When we look at the division within the church over the presentation of the gospel, it is easy to see why even Christians would tend to doubt that such unity could ever come to pass. Let us not forget that with the Lord a day is as a thousand years (see II Peter 3:8); He can do in one day what we might think would take a thousand years. In due time this will happen, and happen swiftly.

However, to prepare for it we must understand how the church departed so far from true unity. When we miss a turn and take the wrong road, it will not turn into the right road just because of good intentions. We need to go back to where we missed the turn and get on the right road. That is called "repentance." This is why we are studying the history of the church while examining our present state. Then we will be able to see our future more clearly.

The Tower of Babel was man's most arrogant attempt to make a name for himself, to gather others around a project, and to reach heaven by his own strength. This is exactly contrary to the plan of God that leads to redemption. He wants men to come to know His name, to gather around His Son, and to reach heaven the way that He has provided. The great sign given on the Day of Pentecost was that it would not be done by man's might or power, but by His Spirit. The church would be God's tower to heaven, and it would gather men together again with a common purpose and a common language, which was the gospel of Jesus Christ.

## THE WRONG TURN

I once heard a man who had just moved to Atlanta say he really appreciated those large signs that showed the way to Interstate 85, but he was just as thankful for the little ones that let him know he was *still on* Interstate 85! God's signs are likewise given to show us the way and to keep us on the way. The first sign given on the day of the church's birth is crucial. Only the Spirit can beget that which is Spirit. Only when Jesus is lifted up can men truly be gathered together. The things that the men of Babel vainly sought in the ways of their fallen nature reflects what God wants to do for men, but these are things only He can do. He does want to unite men, to give them a name, His name, and He does want them to reach into heaven and sit with Him on His throne. However, this can only be done by His Spirit.

After the first century, the church took a wrong turn and actually attempted what the men of Babel had tried to do. Instead of lifting up the name of Jesus, there was a subtle but perceptible drift toward lifting up the name of the church or individual leaders of the church. Then the church was presented as the mediator between God and men which alone could unite men. Ultimately, the church was presented as the way for men to reach heaven. This led to such apostasy that the entire period was called by historians, "The Dark Ages."

Whenever we try to gather men around any other project, regardless of how spiritual or good it seems, even if it is the church, it will ultimately result in men being scattered, rather than gathered. If we are to stay on the way, we must keep seeing the little signs along the way that are there to remind us of this most basic truth—that the church exists for the Lord, not the other way around. If the church is doing its job of lifting up Jesus, she will not be the center of attention, He will.

One can look at the history of the church and see many such towers built by human vanity that we have left in our wake. When the church was essentially united in this foolish task of trying to reach heaven by their own might and power, the Lord again looked down on what we were building and again determined that the only remedy for this tragic folly was to scatter our languages. Now we have thousands of different spiritual languages or denominations, movements, and anti-movements. Because of this, we will never be able to get together in the unity required to finish such vain towers. The only unity that is possible now is the unity around the Son of God.

## THE CRADLE OF THE CHURCH

The culture and conditions in which a person is born and raised will inevitably have a profound impact on the development of their character, and the paradigm from which they view life. Likewise, the culture in which the church was born was obviously intended by God to have a significant influence on its development. The failure to understand the spiritual culture in which the church was born and raised for the first few years was a cause for some of her most devastating mistakes, many of which continue to this day.

The church was born and nurtured in the household of Judaism. Jesus was Jewish. The church was Jewish for the first seven years of its existence. The first disciples continued to follow the basic customs of Judaism. It has been said that a casual observer would have had trouble distinguishing the church from other Jewish sects of the time. In fact, the first apostles considered the church to be an extension of the nation of Israel rather than an entirely new faith for the first two decades of its existence.

Israel was the mother that carried and gave birth to the seed that became Christianity. This was God's purpose when He called Abraham and set aside a people for Himself. God married the mystical nation of Israel and together they had a Son. This is the love story that permeates the Old Testament.

Even though this "mother" became hostile to her own children, the overreaction to this persecution from without and to the Judaisers from within, resulted in more damage to the ultimate development of the church. The church's foundation was still intended to be Jerusalem, not Rome, which it gravitated toward after the severance with Judaism was made.

It was about twenty years after the birth of the church that converts began to consider a significant distinction between themselves and the Jewish nation. This was accomplished mostly through the emergence of a new breed of apostles led by Paul. The brilliant ministry and teachings of Paul helped to make it clear that men could become Christians without passing through the door of Jewish rites. This is quite amazing since Paul had once been one of the most zealous in the strictest Jewish sect, the Pharisees.

## BECOMING BLIND IN ORDER TO SEE

Paul's zeal for the traditions of Judaism had brought him into direct conflict with the truth of the gospel. This caused him to examine those traditions to a much greater degree than it seems any of the others had done. Paul's conversion required that he be struck blind so he could see. This revolutionized his paradigm for viewing truth and ultimately resulted in him developing what is probably the greatest spiritual vision of all time. The most rigid, inflexible zealot became the greatest apostle of grace. Paul will forever be one of the greatest trophies of God's power of redemption.

Though Paul was healed of his blindness after three days, it took time for him to see clearly in the Spirit. As he wrote to the Galatians, he spent fourteen years alone with God in the wilderness searching these matters out. In some ways this strengthened his understanding of the foundation of the gospel, which was established in the Law and the Prophets.

Paul was also able to see where the wrong understanding of the Law and Prophets caused the leaders of Israel to miss the time of their visitation, reject their Messiah, and become opposers of the truth just as he had. This was a strong foundation for his devotion to God's grace. It also enabled him to understand and have compassion for his Jewish brethren who were still trapped in the darkness that had once driven his life.

Like the unfolding of Paul's vision, the transition of the church from being what was considered another Jewish sect to becoming a truly new creation was a gradual process that unfolded over time. Even so, it is apparent that the break from its Jewish roots was never intended to be total. Paul himself made this clear when writing to the Gentile church in Rome.

The book of Romans is considered the most comprehensive exposition of New Covenant theology in the Scriptures, and Paul's explanation of the place of Israel in chapters nine through eleven is a crucial part of this theology. A departure from the warning he gives became the reason for some of the church's greatest mistakes. We would do well to study these chapters over and over. Here I want to direct your attention to the crucial verses of Romans 11:1-32:

I say then, God has not rejected His people, has He? May it never be! For I too am an Israelite, a descendant of Abraham, of the tribe of Benjamin.

God has not rejected His people whom He foreknew. Or do you not know what the Scripture says in the passage about Elijah, how he pleads with God against Israel?

"Lord, they have killed Thy prophets, they have torn down Thine altars, and I alone am left, and they are seeking my life."

But what is the divine response to him? "I have kept for Myself seven thousand men who have not bowed the knee to Baal."

In the same way then, there has also come to be at the present time a remnant according to God's gracious choice.

But if it is by grace, it is no longer on the basis of works, otherwise grace is no longer grace.

What then? That which Israel is seeking for, it has not obtained, but those who were chosen obtained it, and the rest were hardened;

just as it is written, "God gave them a spirit of stupor, eyes to see not and ears to hear not, down to this very day."

And David says, "Let their table become a snare and a trap, and a stumbling block and a retribution to them.

"Let their eyes be darkened to see not, and bend their backs forever."

I say then, they did not stumble so as to fall, did they? May it never be! But by their transgression salvation has come to the Gentiles, to make them jealous.

Now if their transgression be riches for the world and their failure be riches for the Gentiles, how much more will their fulfillment be!

But I am speaking to you who are Gentiles. Inasmuch then as I am an apostle of Gentiles, I magnify my ministry,

if somehow I might move to jealousy my fellow countrymen and save some of them.

For if their rejection be the reconciliation of the world, what will their acceptance be but life from the dead?

And if the first piece of dough be holy, the lump is also; and if the root be holy, the branches are too.

But if some of the branches were broken off, and you, being a wild olive, were grafted in among them and became partaker with them of the rich root of the olive tree,

do not be arrogant toward the branches; but if you are arrogant, remember that it is not you who supports the root, but the root supports you.

You will say then, "Branches were broken off so that I might be grafted in."

Quite right, they were broken off for their unbelief, but you stand by your faith. Do not be conceited, but fear;

for if God did not spare the natural branches, neither will He spare you.

Behold then the kindness and severity of God; to those who fell, severity, but to you, God's kindness, if you continue in His kindness; otherwise you also will be cut off.

And they also, if they do not continue in their unbelief, will be grafted in; for God is able to graft them in again.

For if you were cut off from what is by nature a wild olive tree, and were grafted contrary to nature into a cultivated olive tree, how much more shall these who are the natural branches be grafted into their own olive tree?

For I do not want you, brethren, to be uninformed of this mystery, lest you be wise in your own estimation, that a partial hardening has happened to Israel until the fulness of the Gentiles has come in;

and thus all Israel will be saved; just as it is written, "The Deliverer will come from Zion, He will remove ungodliness from Jacob."

"And this is My covenant with them, when I take away their sins."

From the standpoint of the gospel they are enemies for your sake, but from the standpoint of God's choice they are beloved for the sake of the fathers;

**for the gifts and the calling of God are irrevocable.**

**For just as you once were disobedient to God, but now have been shown mercy because of their disobedience,**

**so these also now have been disobedient, in order that because of the mercy shown to you they also may now be shown mercy.**

**For God has shut up all in disobedience that He might show mercy to all.**

Here we can see that God will never abandon His commitment to Israel. Even though the Jewish people were then enemies of the gospel (verse 28), it was for the church's sake. A partial hardening had come upon the Jews to make them the greatest challenge to the gospel *for the purpose of strengthening the gospel!* It is the nature of true Christianity to thrive with opposition. The worst problems to ever confront the church have come when the world embraced and accepted the church.

As Paul explained to the Romans, the church was called to get so close to God that she would actually provoke the Jews to a godly jealousy so they would be saved. If the church could reach the Jews, then the church could reach the whole world. It was for this reason the church was exhorted to preach to the Jew first, not just in favoritism, but because the ability of their message to reach the Jews was the "acid test" of whether they had the truth. Until we have a faith that makes the Jew jealous, we do not yet have the fullness of what is intended.

It was clearly the Lord's intention to restore **"the natural branches"** (verses 22-32), and to do it through the Gentiles.

The Gentiles received the blessings of the Scriptures and the Messiah through the Jewish people. The Jewish people will receive the blessing of the gospel through the Gentiles. All are in need of mercy and all will receive it including the Jewish people who rejected their own Messiah. God gives His grace to the humble (see James 4:6). It took humility for the Gentiles to receive their grace through the Jewish people, and it will take humility for the Jewish people to receive their grace through the Gentiles.

The most important prophets, kings, and spiritual movements are inevitably born in difficult, hostile conditions. God's ways are contrary to fallen man's ways. His wisdom is far above the greatest human wisdom, but can only be seen through the eyes of true humility which are like a child's. What happened to Judaism to make it oppose the very One for whom they had waited for so many centuries would also happen to Christianity when it "matured," causing the institutional church to one day become an even greater persecutor of the truth than Judaism had been. The same evil has been able to creep into every new spiritual movement so that it would in turn persecute the next movement. This cycle must end, but it will not end until we return to the roots where it began.

Instead of the church seeing the hardened Jews as a challenge to test the quality of their own life and message, the increasingly Gentile church gradually abandoned the commission to go to the Jews first. After the destruction of Jerusalem, the spiritual center of the church gradually moved west until it was centered in Rome. As this happened, all ties to Judaism were severed. Paul's warning not to become arrogant toward the natural branches was forgotten. He had warned that this would result in their being cut off from the root also. This happened as the life and power of the Holy Spirit was gradually substituted with rituals that were foreign to both Judaism and the apostles.

## THE LAW PROPHESIED

The church was called to be the possession of God, His dwelling place. The Law was given to prepare His people for this. However, the Law did not prepare us by making us righteous and holy, but prepared us by revealing the standards of God's righteousness and holiness, and how unrighteous and unholy we are. This revealed how desperately we need His salvation and His power in order to live a holy life.

The Law compels us to flee to the cross for salvation. This is not just for forgiveness, but for deliverance and for power that we might live righteous and holy before Him. The cross does not just extend forgiveness and then leave us in our sin. The cross is also the power of God to live right before Him, which the Law did not have. This basic truth is the reason Paul wrote the book of Galatians.

Even so, there is another purpose for the Law which has seldom been understood. In Matthew 5:18 the Lord made a statement about this purpose for the Law: **"For truly I say to you, until heaven and earth pass away, not the smallest letter or stroke shall pass away from the Law,** *until all is accomplished."* He is not saying here that the Law would not pass away until we have kept all of the commandments, since that would be in conflict with the basic principles of the New Covenant, but He is explaining the Law's purpose in being a *prophecy*. This He also affirmed in Matthew 11:13 when He said: **"For all the prophets and** *the Law prophesied* **until John."**

Not only did it prophesy of the coming of Christ, but it contains in remarkable detail an outline of history. In His great wisdom the Lord knew and foretold even the great mistakes the church would make—her apostasy and her glorious recovery.

All of the rituals and feasts of the Law prophetically portrayed Christ. That is why both the Lord Jesus and the early church continued to observe them. This was not done for righteousness, as our righteousness is gained through the cross alone. However, the first century church continued to observe the rituals of the Law as a celebration of the reality that they had now become fulfilled in Christ. When the church was completely cut off from its Jewish roots, pagan rituals were substituted for those that spoke of Christ, and the drift toward deep darkness ensued.

Modern Christians often forget that the Old Testament was the only Bible the first century church had, and that it was the foundation for the New Testament doctrines of the faith. The apostles used the Law and the Prophets to prove their revelation of the kingdom of God and to prove that Jesus was the promised Messiah, as we see in the texts below:

> **Now to Him who is able to establish you according to my gospel and the preaching of Jesus Christ, according to the revelation of the mystery which has been kept secret for long ages past,**
>
> **but now is manifested, and by the Scriptures of the prophets, according to the commandment of the eternal God, has been made known to all the nations, leading to obedience of faith (Romans 16:25-26).**
>
> **And when they had set a day for him, they came to him at his lodging in large numbers; and he was**

**explaining to them by solemnly testifying about the kingdom of God, and trying to persuade them concerning Jesus, from both the Law of Moses and from the Prophets, from morning until evening (Acts 28:23).**

**"The Scriptures"** that Paul refers to in Romans 16 and in all of his other letters are what we call the Old Testament. They did not have the New Testament when these letters were written. Again, the Old Testament was the only Bible that the early church had, and it was the basis for all of their doctrines and practices, including their revelation of the grace of God through Christ.

We tend to think of the Old Testament as Law and the New Testament as Grace, but this is not necessarily true. The Old Covenant is the Letter, and the New Covenant is by Faith through the Holy Spirit. If you read the New Testament with an Old Covenant heart, it will just be Law to you. Likewise, if you read the Old Testament with a New Covenant heart, you will see Christ in all of it.

The terminology used in the New Testament to describe the place and ministry of the Lord Jesus is from the terminology used in the Law and the Prophets. He is called the High Priest after the Old Testament type who was the Mediator between the nation of Israel and the Lord. He is called **"the Lamb of God"** after the sacrificial lamb which according to the Law was to atone for the sins of the people. That is why Jesus made the astonishing statement in John 5:46-47: **"For if you believed Moses, you would believe Me; for he wrote of Me. But if you do not believe his writings, how will you believe My words?"** He made a similar statement in Luke 24:25-27:

> And He said to them, "O foolish men and slow of heart to believe in all that the prophets have spoken!
>
> "Was it not necessary for the Christ to suffer these things and to enter into His glory?"
>
> And beginning with Moses and with all the prophets, He explained to them the things concerning Himself in all the Scriptures.

We will indeed be foolish if we do not believe *all* that is written in the Law and Prophets. A considerable amount of the foolishness into which the church has fallen can be attributed to our failure in this. We too need to keep in mind the exhortation that Paul gave in II Timothy 3:14-17:

> You, however, continue in the things you have learned and become convinced of, knowing from whom you have learned them;
>
> and that from childhood you have known the sacred writings which are able to give you the wisdom that leads to salvation through faith which is in Christ Jesus.
>
> All Scripture is inspired by God and profitable for teaching, for reproof, for correction, for training in righteousness;
>
> that the man of God may be adequate, equipped for every good work.

Of course, "all Scripture" that Paul is referring to here is what we call the Old Testament. "The Law and the Prophets" was the only Bible the early church had, which was enough for the early church to turn the world upside down. Now we have the New Testament also. The Lord really did save His best wine for last. Even so, the addition of the New Testament was never meant to supplant the purpose of that which we call the Old Testament.

It should be noted that the writer of what is considered the meatiest of the New Testament Epistles, the book of Hebrews, lamented that he could only give the readers milk because they were not ready for solid food! All that is written in Hebrews about Melchizedek, the tabernacle, and the expansive overview of the purposes of God was still spiritual milk and not solid food! How many Christians today even know what the Melchizedek priesthood is? It is the priesthood that we are called to in Christ, so is it not time that we were weaned from milk and go on to solid food? Much of that solid food is found in the Old Testament which can only be seen when it is understood as prophecy.

## ROOT AND BRANCHES

Now how does all of this apply to the distinction between the Jewish and Gentile churches? First, we need to see God's purpose for keeping them distinct and yet one in Christ. Even though they were to be different in many ways, it was the obvious intention of the Lord for the Gentile "branches" of the church to be linked to the Jewish roots, as Paul explained in Romans. Even so, the Gentile "branches" were allowed to establish a church life that was different in many ways from Jewish Christians. This was done with the full blessing and encouragement of the original apostles, verified by the Holy Spirit, and established by the Scriptures. The first Council in Jerusalem confirmed this, and liberated the Gentiles from all of the rituals of the Law, concluding with:

**For it seemed good to the Holy Spirit and to us to lay upon you no greater burden than these essentials:**

**that you abstain from things sacrificed to idols and from blood and from things strangled and from fornication; if you keep yourselves free from such things, you will do well. Farewell (Acts 15:28-29).**

It is often overlooked that this decree was issued specifically for Gentiles and not for Jewish believers. They continued to observe the rituals contained in the Law and the Prophets. As stated, these were now kept as a celebration rather than for righteousness, as the Epistle to the Hebrews makes clear, but it is important for us to see that a distinction is made between what was required of the Jewish and Gentile believers.

A primary stumbling block that keeps many from being able to see this is the concept that Judaism only represents the keeping of the Law for righteousness, which nullifies the grace that we receive through Christ. Many of the first Jewish believers and even some of the Gentile believers also had a hard time making this distinction. Even so, it seems to be the clear intent of the Holy Spirit for the Jewish believers to keep alive the prophetic rituals and celebrations, and then the Gentile church would be free to develop a style that was completely fresh and new. For as long as the Jewish and Gentile believers were linked in fellowship, the important moorings of the church in the historic path of God's redemptive purposes through Israel would be maintained through the Jewish roots of the church.

Another fact that made it clear that the Lord intended for there to be a distinction between the Gentile and Jewish believers was the appointment of an apostle to the Jews and an apostle to the Gentiles. It is also significant that Paul referred to the Gentile "branches," plural, which indicated that there would be diversity within the Gentile groups.

With strong moorings to the Jewish roots, there could be a considerable liberty in the expression of the faith through different cultures and races while still maintaining knowledge of God's righteousness and holiness. With the fresh, creative vitality of the Gentile branches, the Jewish roots would not be as prone to fall back into the rigid inflexibility of the Law. Both are essential, but they had to remain linked to each other while being free to be unique and different.

## SUMMARY

The God who loves diversity so much that He makes every snowflake different, who delights in making people different, obviously intended from the beginning for the church to reflect His glorious creativity. Even so, in Christ we are also to become **"one new man" (Ephesians 2:15)**. Understanding the **"one new man"** in this light has been difficult because we tend to only be able to see unity in conformity instead of the higher unity in diversity. Just as a man does not become one with his wife by making her a man, but by appreciating the differences of the woman, the Jewish and Gentile churches must learn to appreciate the intended differences to come into a true unity in Christ. When this is accomplished it will be a remarkable demonstration of God's will for the unity of all nations through His Son, which is exactly what it will be when it is accomplished at the end of this age.

This is why Paul so resolutely preached that even though the Jews had been hardened to the gospel, they would be grafted in again as **"natural branches" (Romans 11:24)**. This is why the modern "Messianic Jewish" congregations now spreading around the world are so important. Though both the Messianic and Gentile congregations of today are still quite far from the apostolic model of the first century, they are both moving swiftly toward what was intended in the beginning and confirmed by the Council in Jerusalem. At the end this **"one new man"** will be composed of those from every nation.

When this unity between Jew and Gentile is accomplished, it will represent the overcoming of the ultimate racial barriers in the church. Such grace can only come through humility on the part of both the Jews and the Gentiles, which enables each to clearly see the purpose of God for the other. Because God gives His grace to the humble, this will enable the release of unprecedented power to His people, even the power which raises the dead.

## NEXT YEAR IN JERUSALEM?

The overreaction to Judaism by the early church is understandable in the light of three main factors. First was the persecution that the young church endured from traditional Judaism. Second were the problems caused by Jewish converts who tried to impose the Law on the Gentile believers. Third was the destruction of Jerusalem in 70 A.D. When Jerusalem was destroyed it scattered the remaining Jewish apostles and elders, severing most of the links that the Gentile churches had with their Jewish brethren. Now, at the end of this age we are seeing all of these conditions reversed. The nation of Israel has been re-gathered and Jerusalem has again been repossessed by the Jewish people. Multitudes of Messianic Jewish congregations are forming around the world and throughout the land of Israel. We will soon see Jerusalem again become a spiritual center of the faith, just as many biblical prophecies declare.

At the end, the church will again be restored to its strong, Jewish roots and will have strong, Gentile branches. Even so, for the true unity that God desires between the Gentile branches and the Jewish roots, neither will have to compromise their uniqueness. When the joining is right, each will be free to be who God has called them to be. Then the church will truly be a "**... house of prayer for all the nations" (Mark 11:17)** or literally, "a house of prayer for all ethnics."

# CHAPTER EIGHT

# EARLY CHURCH GOVERNMENT

I N THE PREVIOUS CHAPTERS WE EXAMINED THE message and lifestyle of the first century church. In this chapter we will view the church government established by the apostles.

## A GOVERNMENT OF LIBERTY

Church government under the original apostles was so unique, free, and yet so effective that it defied definition. It was such a radical departure from anything the world had ever seen that it was impossible for the world to understand using any authority structure that was presently known. Like the other great principles of the faith, when there is an attempt to overly define it the essence of what it is intended to be is often lost. The first century church government was not dependent on just one form, but on the anointing of the leaders who held the positions. Because of this, it had to be defined by the ones leading more than the system itself.

The apostles did not have a constitution which decreed that they could dictate policy. Their authority came from something much higher—they had been with Jesus and they were anointed by Him. Therefore, the only ones who could recognize their authority had to know the Lord and know the anointing.

The exercise of authority in the first century church was both hierarchical and democratic. The main function of the apostles was to lay a solid foundation of doctrine and to establish a church government which promoted liberty, not conformity. They accomplished this for a time. The freedom this allowed enabled the hearts of men to be converted by the power of truth and the conviction of the Holy Spirit, not by coercion. From the beginning, this was intended to be the mode of operation for the spiritual authority exercised in the church. There was room for discipline and correction, but the ultimate penalty the authorities of the church could exercise was the removal of the offender from fellowship until there was repentance.

The adherence of the apostles to this course of leadership was in such contrast to anything that had been known before, and certainly to the culture of the times, that it constituted the most extraordinary leadership ever exercised by any government at the time. As the church drifted from the genius of this extraordinary style of leadership, oppression grew, and the power of truth was replaced with a terrible, barbaric force intended to compel men to bend their knees to the dictates of church leaders without first bending their hearts to the truth.

## BLESSING TO THE WORLD

When the church began the long process of returning to its original form of church government, the birth of democracy in civil governments and the esteem for human dignity and liberty for all were the immediate results. The great freedom movements of the last five hundred years can all be traced to the teachings of the reformers. Without question, religious liberty is the foundation upon which all true liberty will always be based.

When the Lord placed the Tree of the Knowledge of Good and Evil in the garden, it was not to cause Adam and Eve to fall, but to give them the opportunity to prove their obedience. There can be no true obedience unless there is the freedom to disobey. This is why the gospel is sent out with such humility, carried by earthen vessels. In this age the Lord is calling forth a people to be joint heirs with Him. They will rule and reign with Him over the nations. He will only have in this great position those who come because they love the truth, not because of political expediency or a lust for power.

These will prove their love for the truth by taking their stand for righteousness when it is least expedient, even to the forfeiture of their lives when it is required. These will not have come out of compulsion, but something much deeper—hearts that love God and His ways above all else. Such alone are worthy to be the bride of the Lamb.

## THE FORMS OF GOVERNMENT

As much as we may be repelled at the abuses of hierarchical forms of church government, and as much as this form of government has been used to stifle liberty, it was unquestionably an aspect of New Testament church government. However, one can also use the New Testament to make a case for having co-equal elders as a government for the church. Both forms of government have merits and biblical precedents. What we cannot say is that either form is *the* New Testament form of church government. It seems that even in the form of church government that we use, the Lord intended for us to have liberty and diversity. This will seem impractical to the natural mind, but for true spiritual development it is essential.

Even the best form of government will be bad government without good people in it. Likewise, the worst form of government can be good government if it has good people in it. If we want good government, we cannot over-emphasize the form. Nevertheless, our goal should be to have good, qualified people in leadership with the best form of government that will be an aid and not a hindrance to the anointing of that particular group.

As we read the New Testament, it seems as if the form of church government used just evolved over time. This is an accurate depiction. The Lord was building His government around people—not trying to build people around a form of government.

This is not to imply that the Lord did not know where He was going with this. However, when too much government is imposed on people prematurely, it can stifle true spiritual development. On the other hand, when a group is young they will probably need more controls than when they are more mature. This is a very delicate balance and there will certainly be a temptation to just impose what brings control. However, if we are truly wise we will be careful, patient, and flexible in imposing a government on a new church or movement. In this way, the anointing that is in the people can give definition to the government.

The Lord always works from the inside out, not the outside in. If our overwhelming emphasis is on imposing a form of government and getting the church to fit into it, at best we are going to end up causing a lot of pain. Government is important. One of the great evils of the last days is lawlessness. Even so, how the government is imposed can be a great help or hindrance to the work. Some people need much more structure in church government than others, and we have the liberty in the New Testament to build this way. When less structure is needed, we also have that liberty.

## A FLEXIBLE WINESKIN

The New Testament church government was intended to be flexible enough to change as the church grew. People who have lived under oppressive forms of government, such as communism, can have their own "decision maker" so broken or underdeveloped that too much liberty can be destructive and confusing to their walk in the Lord. In these cases, liberty must be given gradually.

In contrast to this, some countries where liberty has bordered on lawlessness, almost any exercise of church authority will be viewed as an imposition of a control spirit. This will cause serious rebellion that could have been avoided if authority had been taken more gradually. In places where there is a good balance between liberty and control (not a control spirit), very little government may be needed.

In all cases, church government is intended to help us grow in our submission to the Headship of Jesus. Our goal should always be to promote the individual's personal relationship to the Lord, their ability to know His voice, and their commitment to follow Him. We have church government so that every one of God's people can grow to have the law written in their heart. If we do not keep this ultimate goal in mind, our form of government will fail, regardless of what form it is. This was the true pattern that was left to us by the first century apostles.

## THE REALMS OF AUTHORITY

Jesus is the Head of His church. There is no other leader on earth that can presume that position. He alone is *the* Authority over the entire church. The apostles were the first appointed officers of the church and they were its highest authority on earth. However, apostolic authority was not universal. Paul explained this when he wrote to the Corinthians that: **"if to others I am not an apostle, at least I am to you, for you are the seal of my apostleship in the Lord" (I Corinthians 9:2).** By this he was saying that he was not an apostle to everyone, but he was to the Corinthians because they were a fruit of his apostolic ministry.

When Paul went to Jerusalem he was honored as an apostle to the Gentiles, but he was not received as an apostle to the Jews, and he did not try to exercise apostolic authority in Jerusalem. In some places you can be received as an apostle, in others maybe as a teacher—just as a pastor over one congregation cannot impose his pastoral authority over other congregations. We must recognize the limits of our authority in every situation and stay within them. If we do not, our rejection will not be the result of hardhearted people as much as by our own presumption.

Likewise, Peter was not an apostle to the Gentiles, even though he was used to open the door of the gospel to them. When he went to the Gentiles at Antioch he got into trouble, and Paul, who was called to the Gentiles, had to rebuke him (see Galatians 2:11). This probably happened because Peter was no longer in his realm of authority. When we leave our realm of authority, we depart from the realm of grace which we have been given. Peter just did not have the grace to minister among the Gentiles because he was called to the Jews.

Likewise, when Paul went to the Jews in Jerusalem, he got into trouble. This is hard for some to accept because Paul is almost worshiped as infallible. There was an easier way for him to get to Rome than to go in chains. The Holy Spirit repeatedly warned him not to go to Jerusalem, but Paul had the authority to choose (see Acts 22:17-30). Regardless of whether we think Paul made a mistake or not, the principle is still true, that apostles have realms of authority. If we go beyond our realms of authority, we have gone beyond the grace that we have been given and we will have troubles.

It is important here to reiterate the point that even though Peter was used to open the door of faith to the Gentiles, he was not called to them. Just because you are used to start something does not mean you have authority there. When Mary, the mother of Jesus, came to Him, He responded that His mother and brothers and sisters were those who did the will of God (see Mark 3:31-35). He was saying this to let it be known that just because she gave birth to Him, this did not give her the right to control Him. Not understanding this one point about spiritual authority has caused considerable trouble for the church. When we become possessive, we will probably depart from our appointed realm of authority.

## APOSTOLIC GOVERNMENT

Some have the concept that the ultimate unity of the church can only come from being under one church government. This is both a superficial and a dangerous concept. We will not come into our ultimate unity until we all come under the Headship of Jesus, but true unity will be one of a unity in diversity, not a unity of conformity, especially in church government.

## NEW WINE

There are numerous apostolic movements now being raised up around the world. Some are unique, which can be a testimony to authenticity, but just being unique does not make us apostolic. Even so, one of the banes of modern Christianity has been the tendency of unanointed people trying to gain influence and followers in the church by copying anointed people. Living water only comes out of the innermost being, the heart. Parrots may be able to copy what we say, but it is not in their heart. A true apostolic movement or government must come from what the Lord has deposited in the heart of the apostle, not by his ability to copy others well. This is especially true as it relates to church government.

When true unity comes, all of the apostolic movements should appreciate the uniqueness of the others, embracing a proper level of interchange, but not feeling compelled to be like others. We must have the freedom to be unique if we are ever going to be the body of Christ that we have been called to be. If we are going to be such a body, we do not need to all be hands, eyes, or any other part. Each of us needs to be unique and different, but function together. This is why it is so fundamentally important that there be a restoration and recognition of Jewish roots and Gentile branches. True unity is a unity of diversity, not conformity.

## POSITIONS BASED ON FUNCTION

In the first century all authority in the church was derived from the apostles. This was hierarchical regardless of how much we may want to resist that principle. Even so, the way in which they exercised their authority was to transfer it to any worthy subordinate at every opportunity. Authority was not considered a position of privilege as much as a responsibility to be used for service.

When the position of deacon was instituted, the apostles allowed the congregation to choose those who were to serve with this honor. Regardless of how we would like to view this, it was a remarkable example of democracy in church government. Just as Peter was to later write, the apostles did not act as if they were lords of God's inheritance, but led by being examples to the flock (see I Peter 5:3). They took authority when it was needed, but they seemed to always be devoted to delegating it to the people when possible. If these people were to one day rule over angels, should they not be able to take responsibility in earthly matters?

## TEAM MINISTRY

The apostles were the first ministry established by the Lord, but as they laid a foundation in the church with their teaching and leadership, other ministries began to emerge. Each of these specialized in an aspect of the apostolic ministry. The apostles were all prophets, evangelists, pastors, and teachers, at least to some degree. The emerging ministries from the church mostly specialized in just one of the equipping functions. Some focused on evangelism, others teaching, others the prophetic, administration, or healing, etc. In this way the ministry that had begun with twelve grew throughout the expanding church, meeting the growing needs. The Holy Spirit brought forth gifts and ministries in each so that every believer had a part in the overall ministry of the church.

As we read the book of Acts, it seems that all of this happened quite swiftly, but actually it took many years to unfold. For example, it was seven years from the day that the Holy Spirit was poured out at Pentecost until Peter first preached to the Gentiles in the house of Cornelius. It was more than two decades from the outpouring of the Holy Spirit until Paul and Barnabas were sent out from Antioch.

## MAKE THE CLOTHES TO FIT THE BABY

This unfolding definition of the church is a good pattern for church life, if it is not going to be artificial. When you have a baby you may know it is male or female, but you really will not know what the baby will look like as an adult until he or she has matured. The same is true of the church. For centuries, unfolding movements in the church have often been made to try and fit into clothes that were made for them before they were even born, rather than the church having wisdom to wait to make the clothes after they had matured.

As stated, throughout the Lord's ministry on earth He only made a couple of brief mentions of the church and gave very little definition to what it would be like. Even though He spent many days after His resurrection sharing with His disciples concerning the kingdom, it seems that He actually gave them very little, practical guidance concerning the administration of the church. It is obvious that He purposely wanted them to get this from the Holy Spirit. The Holy Spirit seemed to only give this wisdom when the church needed it, so the structure of the church unfolded over time. In this way, the brilliance of what unfolded was far beyond human genius and it perfectly fit the needs at each stage of development. It may have been much simpler to just impose an unyielding model of government in the beginning, but it would not have been nearly as effective.

As the ministries emerged, a comprehensive team began to form. Prophets began to work closely with the apostles. The pastors and teachers worked closely together. The only evangelist mentioned in the New Testament, Philip, seemed to work alone, but apostles were sent to follow up his work. Local elders were appointed in each congregation to provide guidance and protection in the absence of the apostles, which was most of the time. Together this structure of leadership and responsibility represented an innovation in organization such as the world had never seen. It soon became so powerful that it challenged the very existence of the most powerful institutions and governments on earth.

The New Testament Epistles reveal a number of examples when the apostles dictated policy or took severe action against sin or false doctrines that encroached on the church. Even so, when we see Paul issuing instructions for disciplinary action to the Corinthian church, he did not just address the elders but rather the entire congregation. Basically, the apostles treated believers as if they were fellow heirs, and also kings and priests to God. All believers were therefore treated with the utmost respect. Even so, clear lines of authority were established in the first century church as we see in I Corinthians 12:27-31:

**Now you are Christ's body, and individually members of it.**

**And God has appointed in the church, first apostles, second prophets, third teachers, then miracles, then gifts of healings, helps, administrations, various kinds of tongues.**

**All are not apostles, are they? All are not prophets, are they? All are not teachers, are they? All are not workers of miracles, are they?**

**All do not have gifts of healings, do they? All do not speak with tongues, do they? All do not interpret, do they?**

**But earnestly desire the greater gifts. And I show you a still more excellent way.**

Here we see a clear chain of authority and yet the believers are exhorted to **"desire the greater gifts."** They are reminded that all do not have the same authority, but that they could seek it. The Lord called Paul from being one of the greatest enemies of the church to being one of its greatest leaders, which seemed to show His delight in using His leaders as demonstrations of His power of redemption. The small and the weak, and even the base, were often special qualifications for the ones the Lord wanted to use (see I Corinthians 1:26-29). One of God's main purposes for the church was for her to be an instrument through which He could reach to redeem and restore the lost. Those who were the most in touch with redemption and restoration were the most qualified to carry authority in His church.

## ELDERS

The elders were the highest local authority in a church. This office was borrowed from Israel's government, which had been established by Moses in the wilderness. In Israel there were basically two classes of elders. Because of the Law's admonition to honor fathers and mothers, as well as other biblical exhortations to respect the aged, all of the elderly were given honor and influence in the affairs of the community. However, just as Moses chose seventy **"elders of Israel" (Numbers 11:16)** to exercise governing authority, governing elders in the church were distinguished from those who were simply due respect for their age and faithfulness.

After Israel entered the Promised Land and possessed cities in which to live, a primary responsibility of the governing elders was to sit in the gates of the city. Here they acted as judges and determined who would be allowed to come in or go out of the city. Each gate into the city had a different function. Some were for the merchants to use, others for the soldiers, or nobility, etc. Each elder could exercise authority over different aspects of the city's life because of the gate at which he sat.

This has an important application in the New Testament. Because elders are always mentioned as plural, it can be assumed that elders are always intended to function in plurality. Some have assumed that plurality implies that elders were all equal in authority, but both the Old Testament type and New Testament examples indicate that this is not the case. Elders who sat in one gate did not have the authority to dictate policy over other gates. These may seem like small points, but in their application in the church they can have major consequences.

For example, if we choose someone to be an elder because of his maturity or the respect that he has in the community of believers but he has not been given a specific function, he could easily become a hindrance to the progress of the church, even if he has the best of intentions. Before someone is appointed a "governing elder" we should look for the evidence of God's anointing on them. With the elders Moses chose, the Spirit came upon them and they prophesied.

This may not be exactly how the Lord verifies every elder, but we do need to recognize the Spirit upon them for government. If we appoint someone to this position just to honor them, we will probably pay a high price for it later.

## OTHER SPHERES OF AUTHORITY

Another important point here is to determine just what "gate" the governing elders are called to sit in. Should one who is anointed to oversee church finances have authority over the children's ministry where he may have no anointing or experience? It seems that a modern example of what the presbytery of the church is intended to be like is our Presidential Cabinet. Here we have the heads of the different departments of government sitting in a council where the Secretary of Defense may in fact have some wisdom for the Department of Labor, but he does not have the authority to dictate policy there. Elders may have wisdom for other ministries in the church, but one who is an overseer of one "gate," or ministry should not be able to dictate authority over someone else's sphere of authority.

Of course, important doctrinal issues may arise that do involve the entire church, such as we see in Acts 15. This required a council of all of the apostles and elders. After listening to testimonies and debate, James, who was recognized as the leading elder in Jerusalem, made the decisive statement to decide the issue (verses 13-19). As this **"seemed good"** to the other apostles and elders, a decree was issued concluding the council.

Another sphere of authority for elders can be tied to geography. When Paul talked about his sphere of authority, it was in relation to geographical boundaries (see II Corinthians 10:13-16). Because the Lord established cultures, races, and nations, He prepares special ministries to relate to them. There is likewise a sensitivity to these that everyone in ministry should have, which is why Paul said when he was in Rome he did like the Romans, or when he was with the Jews, he became as a Jew (see I Corinthians 9:20). We do not want our personalities to become *unnecessary* stumbling blocks to the gospel. Many of the unnecessary offenses that have come to Christianity have come because we have failed to walk in this wisdom or have tried to go beyond the realm of authority which has been given to us geographically.

We should also recognize that when Peter and John referred to themselves as elders, they were not talking about being elders in a local church or even in the foundational church of Jerusalem. Peter and John were both recognized as elders of the whole body of Christ. Does this not conflict with the statement that the Lord alone is Head of the whole church? No. There are realms of authority that are international and some may even extend to the whole church, but in specific areas of influence, not headship.

Being respected in such a capacity does not give one the authority to dictate policy over the entire church. But these men and women have or are beginning to sit in gates or spiritual doors that are releasing something into large sections of the church. There are many others who have international ministries. And, although some of them may have both age and longevity in that position, they just do not carry the kind of authority that would cause us to recognize them as elders of the entire body of Christ.

We can biblically recognize elders on the local church level and the international level, but does this mean we can have elders positioned in levels in-between these? To be a biblical people does not mean that we cannot do anything unless we find it specifically written in the Scriptures, but it means we have the liberty to do it if it does not specifically violate what is written. This does not mean anything we do that does not violate Scripture is right, but that we are free to be led by the Holy Spirit in these matters. I personally think it is right to recognize elders on every level of authority in which we are ministering. This would include recognizing elders in specific positions within movements.

Was there meant to be a hierarchy among elders? The only hierarchy mentioned in Scripture is that the apostles had authority over the elders and elders had authority over the church, including the deacons. The same Greek word is used for both bishop and presbyter in the New Testament and was obviously referring to the same office in the apostolic writings. The elevation of the office of bishop above that of presbyter was done gradually and was not recognized in church government until sometime between 70 and 120 A.D.

Emerging movements today use titles for the same function that range from "leading elder" to apostle. Biblically we cannot establish that they had any extra local authority in the church except for apostles and prophets, or elders that sat in special councils with the apostles, such as we see in the council in Jerusalem.

## THE GOOSE PRINCIPLE

Geese are remarkable birds with a form of government in each flock. This government is popularly known as "the pecking order." Every goose in the flock knows his or her place. For a goose to rise out of their place in the flock, they will have to fight and subdue a goose that is on a level above them. This may sound brutal, but it is in reality the way most human groups also act.

Geese always fly in formation, but it has a very different purpose than the ability of one goose to dominate another. They fly in formation in order to help one another. The lead goose is actually doing the most work, being the servant of the others. In flight, the lead goose must cut through the wind while all of the others are drafting behind each other. By drafting this way, all but the lead goose are using 20 to 35 percent less effort than the leader. Therefore, the leader will tire much more quickly than the others. This requires a constant changing of leadership if the flock is to keep pace.

When I inquired of the Lord how we could create a church or movement that would not stop moving, I was told that I needed to observe the wisdom of the geese. While earthbound, there will always be bickering and infighting about who is positioned where. However, as long as we are going somewhere, whoever is in leadership will not matter as much as keeping pace and keeping on course.

I believe this is biblical too. It seems that just in the first century we see the leadership of the church going from Peter, to James, to Paul, and then to John. In the church today we see ministries emerge that help take the whole church a little further and then they seem to give way to another one. Some of this is fad chasing, but some of it is the Holy Spirit keeping us moving forward.

## STAYING FRESH

We have also started to apply this in our local church. We now have three main worship leaders who I think could be classified as "chief musicians." We then have about a dozen who are emerging and lead from time to time—some of whom we think will be chief musicians. This has brought a vitality and diversity to our worship which has caused me to believe that we could have continually fresh and creatively advancing worship.

We have also done this with the preaching and teaching in the church. I am the overseer of the congregation, but we have many outstanding preachers and teachers on staff who all take turns in the pulpit. This has brought a freshness and vitality to the church which I think has been a major contributing factor to enabling some of our local church meetings to exceed anything we have experienced in conferences. Just two years ago I did not think that was possible. In almost every service we give ten to fifteen minutes to someone to speak from the congregation or school of ministry. These have been so good that the congregation now has a genuine expectancy and excitement when they see someone about to speak that they have not heard before.

We are also implementing this in every department of the church. For example, when our pastor over the children's ministry began to become weary, we moved someone else into the leadership position there and the former pastor took his place behind the new leader. There was some resistance to this at first, but there was an immediate acceleration in the children's ministry. Within weeks the former leader was thanking us. We have let everyone know that when he is rested and his vision renewed he may lead again, unless the Lord directs someone else into the position.

There are also three other departments (or gates) in our ministry in which we have or are now implementing such changes. Everyone in the ministry, including myself, knows that when we tire, and things begin to bog down, a change is coming. We must do this if we are going to continue moving forward. True leaders who are true servants will always welcome this.

Is this not the model that was given us in the Levitical priesthood? They ministered in the tabernacle from the time that they were thirty until they were fifty and then they allowed the next generation to take over. This kept the ministry fresh. Those who were removed from ministry at age fifty were not just put out to pasture, but entered some of the most fruitful years of their lives discipling the emerging generation, and taking their place as elders in the gates.

In the New Testament, a distinction is made between the authority that one exercises as one of the equipping ministries such as apostle, prophet, evangelist, pastor, or teacher, and the authority of an elder. We must also observe that the ministry of the pastor is only mentioned one time in the New Testament when listed with the others in Ephesians Four, and yet somehow it has come to almost completely dominate the ministry of the modern church! It was obviously only intended to be one member of a team of ministries given for the equipping of the people, who were themselves to do the work of the ministry.

## SUMMARY

If we really want to comply with the biblical models of church government, radical changes must come to most modern churches and movements. It is also obvious that they are coming. Many new movements are now sweeping across the church. They are coming with such life and vitality that they are forcing change by their very existence. The inability to accept change is a characteristic of those who have become an old wineskin. The Lord is seeking to prepare a wineskin that is perpetually flexible enough to embrace the new wine.

The government of the New Testament church was the most innovative and flexible system of authority ever devised. It was a blend of both hierarchy and democracy, promoting both liberty and order at the same time. Those who have been able to resist adding or taking away from it have a perfect framework which the Spirit of God can use. Yet, it is also a framework for the initiative and disciplinary measures that will always be needed and taken from time to time.

The Lord could have been much more specific in making a clear outline for church government in the Scriptures. However, what He did give us makes and allows us to be dependent on the Holy Spirit for many possible applications. This is obviously very important for true church life as it is intended to be. God does not anoint a position, but a person. We can have all of the positions, but if we do not have anointed people in them, they will be miserable failures at administrating the church. Likewise, we can have wrong positions or even no positions, but if someone with the anointing comes there will be authority. However, what we need to seek is both the right positions and the right people.

# CHAPTER NINE

# PERSECUTION AND PERSERVERANCE

I N THIS CHAPTER WE EXAMINE THE EFFECT THAT persecution had on the development of the Christian faith and how we can expect it to effect the last day church.

In the first century, Christianity was a supernatural experience. God is supernatural. If we are going to experience God, it will be a supernatural experience. If we are going to walk with God, we must become comfortable with the supernatural. In the early church the Lord Himself appeared to people at times. There were interchanges with angels to the degree that the church was exhorted to be careful how they treated strangers because they could be angels (see Hebrews 13:2). The Lord was very close to His people and the spiritual realm became familiar to all believers. This made it easier for them to endure the almost continual opposition, persecution, and afflictions.

The Scriptures make it clear that it will be the same at the end of the age, with both the supernatural characteristics of Christianity and the tribulations. Church leaders from the first century have understood this to be **"the early and** latter rain" (Joel 2:23). We also see this in Acts 2:17-21, which Peter quoted from the book of Joel:

**"And it shall be in the last days," God says, "That I will pour forth of My Spirit upon all mankind; and your sons and your daughters shall prophesy, and your young men shall see visions, and your old men shall dream dreams;**

**Even upon My bondslaves, both men and women, I will in those days pour forth of My Spirit and they shall prophesy.**

**"And I will grant wonders in the sky above, and signs on the earth beneath, blood, and fire, and vapor of smoke.**

**"The sun shall be turned into darkness, and the moon into blood, before the great and glorious day of the Lord shall come.**

**"And it shall be, that everyone who calls on the name of the Lord shall be saved."**

The verses above show us that when the Lord pours out His Spirit there will be prophecy, dreams, and visions. This will obviously be increased in the last days because we are going to need it then. As Paul explained to the disciples, **"Through many tribulations we must enter the kingdom of God" (Acts 14:22).** This was a proven truth in the first century. The more the church was afflicted, the more spiritual authority they experienced. Quickly they learned to be thankful for all such trials because they prepared them to be stewards of even greater power.

## BATTLES ON EVERY SIDE

Everything about the young church seemed especially designed to draw wrath from all of the prevailing powers on the earth. The religious leaders of the time felt threatened by any group that represented change, or one which they could not control. They had been known to use almost any means to silence those who challenged their dominance. They would even hire false witnesses to bring charges against them, or turn them over to the hated Romans for their oppressive powers. On a whim, they could exile a person from the synagogue, which meant that this person could not trade or relate to anyone in the community, effectively driving them from their homes, their families, and their country.

The religious oppression of the first century Israel could be as stifling as the political and military oppression of Rome. It was a difficult time to embrace any kind of new movement that was perceived to be a challenge to the status quo.

To call Jesus Lord also incited the Roman officials, who considered it an affront to the authority of the Emperor. This would ultimately release against the young church the cruelest persecutions yet experienced in the civilized world. To become a Christian marked one as a special target for persecutions and afflictions that could come at any time from any number of directions. Thus, to become a Christian also marked one as a part of a community whose courage was unprecedented.

Never had a people arisen who were willing to suffer so much for the sake of their beliefs. The truth for which they lived was so great that they were also willing to die for it. Nothing like this had been seen on the earth before. For nearly three centuries, to believe in Jesus meant risking your life every day. The Lord Jesus had warned His disciples that this would be their lot just as it was His:

"Behold, I send you out as sheep in the midst of wolves; therefore be shrewd as serpents, and innocent as doves.

"But beware of men; for they will deliver you up to the courts, and scourge you in their synagogues;

and you shall even be brought before governors and kings for My sake, as a testimony to them and to the Gentiles.

"But when they deliver you up, do not become anxious about how or what you will speak; for it shall be given you in that hour what you are to speak.

"For it is not you who speak, but it is the Spirit of your Father who speaks in you.

"And brother will deliver up brother to death, and a father his child; and children will rise up against parents, and cause them to be put to death.

"And you will be hated by all on account of My name, but it is the one who has endured to the end who will be saved.

"But whenever they persecute you in this city, flee to the next; for truly I say to you, you shall not finish going through the cities of Israel, until the Son of Man comes.

"A disciple is not above his teacher, nor a slave above his master.

"It is enough for the disciple that he become as his teacher, and the slave as his master. If they have called the head of the house Beelzebul, how much more the members of his household!

"Therefore do not fear them, for there is nothing covered that will not be revealed, and hidden that will not be known.

"What I tell you in the darkness, speak in the light; and what you hear whispered in your ear, proclaim upon the housetops.

"And do not fear those who kill the body, but are unable to kill the soul; but rather fear Him who is able to destroy both soul and body in hell.

"Are not two sparrows sold for a cent? And yet not one of them will fall to the ground apart from your Father.

"But the very hairs of your head are all numbered.

"Therefore do not fear; you are of more value than many sparrows.

"Everyone therefore who shall confess Me before men, I will also confess him before My Father who is in heaven.

"But whoever shall deny Me before men, I will also deny him before My Father who is in heaven.

"Do not think that I came to bring peace on the earth; I did not come to bring peace, but a sword.

"For I came to set a man against his father, and a daughter against her mother, and a daughter-in-law against her mother-in-law;

**and a man's enemies will be the members of his household.**

**"He who loves father or mother more than Me is not worthy of Me; and he who loves son or daughter more than Me is not worthy of Me.**

**"And he who does not take his cross and follow after Me is not worthy of Me.**

**"He who has found his life shall lose it, and he who has lost his life for My sake shall find it (Matthew 10:16-39).**

As the book of Acts documents, the early church was born in persecution and with the exception of some brief respites, grew and prospered in the midst of continual opposition. Diabolical rumors about Christians were devised and spread throughout the empire. The Christian "love-feasts" and celebrations of the Lord's Supper were declared to be a covering for the most hideous crimes. Misunderstanding the ritual symbolism of communion, the partaking of the body and blood of Christ, the report was fostered that at such gatherings Christians would bind themselves into a criminal league by making a feast upon a slaughtered child, and then give themselves up to the most shameless indulgence.

The rumor that Christians were cannibals persisted for centuries. There was such a revulsion to what was claimed that Christians practiced in private, soon every public calamity was attributed to them. This charge of cannibalism also justified to the Romans the act of feeding Christians to wild beasts which for a time became a sport in major cities. Christians were hung on crosses, dipped in oil and burned, sometimes even used as streetlights. Hideous tortures were devised as the Roman Emperor Nero unleashed the full power of the imperial sword in an attempt to destroy the young church.

## THE MORE THEY DIED, THE STRONGER THEY BECAME

To the great consternation of the Roman and religious officials of the time, the more they afflicted the young church, the more it grew and spread abroad. Every time a church was scattered, the people became like seed and dozens of other congregations would sprout up. When one leader was killed, a dozen would arise to take his place. The Romans could defeat any army in the world, but they could not defeat the truth.

The more severe the persecution, the more grace was extended to the church by the Lord. Just as the first Christian martyr, Stephen, had beheld the glory of the Lord as he was being stoned, seemingly not even aware of the mortal wounds being afflicted upon him, martyrs who were tortured by the Romans experienced such grace that they did not even seem to feel the pain of their afflictions. The peace and glory reflected from them was so great that at times their torturers were converted on the spot, choosing to embrace the same kind of death for the sake of the truth found in Christ.

Many who came to watch the Christians be devoured by lions were so stunned by their courage that they could find no peace until they, too, embraced faith in Christ. Nothing had ever been seen anywhere in the world like this. It defied any human explanation.

## THE PERSEVERANCE OF THE SAINTS

These persecutions against the church did not just last a few months or even years, but for almost three centuries!

The most intense persecution of all came during the last ten years of this period. On February 24, 303, an imperial decree was issued requiring the destruction of all Christian property, all copies of the Bible, and a reduction of all Christians to the status of slaves. With these civil rights revoked, the entire populace of the empire was free to attack and afflict Christians in any way they desired. Their property was seized, their persons violated in every conceivable way, and multitudes were slaughtered. Yet, the faith continued to spread and prevail, and the faithful grew even bolder in their witness.

Opposition can never hurt the truth; it can only help to purify it and make it stronger. During such times of persecution there were no false conversions. Because leaders became special targets, those who accepted leadership positions were not motivated by selfish ambition, but only out of a sincere love for the Lord and His people. Many of the petty issues that would later cause division in the church in times of peace could find no place to produce discord in the persecuted church. Persecution was the fire that consumed the wood, hay, and stubble, and purified the gold, silver, and precious stones.

As Paul wrote to his son in the faith, Timothy, **"And indeed, all who desire to live godly in Christ Jesus will be persecuted" (II Timothy 3:12).** As Jesus had said, **"Blessed are those who have been persecuted for the sake of righteousness, for theirs is the kingdom of heaven. "Blessed are you when men cast insults at you, and persecute you, and say all kinds of evil against you falsely, on account of Me. Rejoice, and be glad, for your reward in heaven is great, for so they persecuted the prophets who were before you" (Matthew 5:10-12).** When viewing the procession of the church through history, it is apparent that persecution is the "normal" state of the truly faithful.

## WE TOO HAVE A CUP TO DRINK

True Christianity has always been an affront and a threat to those who live by the ways of this present, evil world, including professing Christians who have compromised with the ways of the world. This should never be a shock or a discouragement to us, but rather be expected. In fact, we should be more concerned when we are not being persecuted because it can be a sign that we are not really living godly in Christ Jesus and are therefore not a threat to the powers of darkness.

Persecution has a way of stripping away all of the facades and pretenses in order to reduce our faith and our lives to what we really believe and hold essential. Those who believe the truth of the gospel will not compromise it even if it means giving up their life.

The truth of the gospel *is* more important than this life. As a testimony to this, every one of the original twelve apostles died a martyr's death with the possible exception of John, whose death was not recorded in history. The following accounts were condensed from *Foxe's Book of Martyrs,* and the accounts of Jerome, Clement, and other early church fathers. These accounts are traditions that were passed down rather than eyewitness reports. However, they are corroborated by so many that it is likely they are at least relatively accurate.

## THE MARTYRDOM OF THE APOSTLES

After the martyrdom of Stephen, James, the brother of John, suffered next. Clement wrote that when James was brought to the tribunal seat, it was the man who was the cause of his trouble that brought him there. While seeing James condemned to suffer death, he was so moved by remorse that as he went to James' execution, he confessed Christ himself so that they were led forth together. On the way he asked James to forgive him what he had done. James paused, then replied, "Peace be to you, brother," and kissed him. They were beheaded together in 36 A.D.

Thomas preached to the Parthians, Medes, Persians, Carmanians, Hyrcanians, Bactrians, and Magians. In Calamina, a city of India, he was slain with an arrow.

Simon, who was the brother of Jude and James the Younger, who all were the sons of Mary Cleophas and of Alpheus, became the Bishop of Jerusalem after James. Simon was crucified in a city of Egypt in the time of Trajan the Emperor.

Simon the apostle, called Cananeus and Zelotes, preached in Mauritania, and in the country of Africa, and in Britain where he was crucified.

Mark, the evangelist and first Bishop of Alexandria, preached the gospel in Egypt, and was drawn with ropes there, which pulled all of the joints out of their sockets. Then he was set on fire. This happened during the reign of Trajan.

Bartholomew is said also to have preached to the Indians and to have translated the Gospel of Matthew into their language. In Albinopolis, a city of greater Armenia, he was beaten with staves, crucified, and then beheaded.

Andrew, the brother to Peter, was crucified by Aegeas, a Roman governor, in a city which is called Sebastopolis. Andrew, through his preaching, had brought so many to faith in Christ that the governor came to the province to compel them to sacrifice to idols and renounce the faith. Andrew challenged Aegeas to his face, calling him to renounce his false gods and idols, declaring that the gods and idols of the Romans were not gods, but devils and the enemies of mankind. In a rage, the proconsul charged Andrew not to teach and preach such things any more and if he did he would be fastened to the cross with all speed. Andrew replied, "I would not have preached the honor and glory of the cross, if I feared the death of the cross." Andrew was immediately condemned.

As Andrew was being taken to the place of his execution, seeing the cross being prepared in the distance, he cried out, "O cross, most welcome and long looked for! With a willing mind, joyfully and desirously, I come to thee, being the scholar of Him which did hang on thee: because I have always been thy lover, and have coveted to embrace thee."

Matthew, also called Levi, after he had converted many from Aethiopia and seemingly all of Egypt to the faith, their king, Hircanus, ran him through with a spear.

Philip, the apostle, after he had labored preaching the Word to some of the most barbarous nations of the time, was crucified and stoned in Hierapolis, a city of Phrygia.

James, the brother of the Lord, was esteemed by all of Jerusalem for his righteousness, being called "James the Just." When many of the chief men of the city believed, the leading scribes and Pharisees ordered James to restrain the people from believing that Jesus was the Messiah. During the Passover, they carried him to a battlement on the temple from which he could address the crowds below. When James began to testify that Jesus was the Christ and was at that time sitting at the right hand of the Father, he was thrown from the top. He did not die immediately, but struggled to his knees to pray for his persecutors. They rushed down and began to stone him. He continued his prayers as Stephen had done before him, until he died.

Peter was preaching in Rome when he was entreated to flee the city because Nero sought to put him to death. As he was leaving through the gate, he saw a vision of the Lord coming to meet him. Falling to worship Him, Peter asked the Lord where He was going and He responded that He had come to be crucified again. Peter understood that this meant it was his time to follow his Lord in death and he returned to the city. When captured, Peter asked to be crucified upside down because he was not worthy to be crucified in the same manner as the Lord. His request was granted.

Paul, the apostle, was also martyred by Nero. Nero sent two of his own esquires, Ferega and Parthemius, to Paul with the declaration of his sentence of death. Paul prayed for them at their request and told them that they would believe and be baptized at his sepulcher. He was then taken out of the city and beheaded. The two esquires believed.

The persecution ceased under the Emperor Vespasian, but began again under Domitian, the brother of Titus. In this persecution, John, the apostle, was exiled to the island of Patmos. After the death of Domitian, John was released. He then went to Ephesus, where he remained until the time of Trajan. There he sat as an elder to the churches and wrote his Gospel. There are accounts of John's ministry continuing until he reached the age of one hundred. There are also several accounts of attempts being made by the Romans to kill John, but none of them were successful. One states that he was boiled in oil without effect before his exile to Patmos. Because there is no account of his death, it has caused some to wonder about the Lord's statement concerning John that was made to Peter:

> **Peter therefore seeing him said to Jesus, "Lord, and what about this man?"**
>
> **Jesus said to him, "If I want him to remain until I come, what is that to you? You follow Me!"**
>
> **This saying therefore went out among the brethren that that disciple would not die; yet Jesus did not say to him that he would not die, but only, "If I want him to remain until I come, what is that to you?" (John 21:21-23)**

## THEY LOVED NOT THEIR LIVES UNTO DEATH

It was obviously a blow for the young church to see her leaders put to death. Even so, she did not waver, but continued to grow stronger and the gospel continued to spread. Seeing that just killing the leaders could not stop Christianity, the Romans then turned to a general persecution against all who called on the name of the Lord. In some cities it was reported that thousands were put to death every day. At times even the Roman officials were appalled at the slaughter, commenting that the Christians had done nothing worthy of such persecution. Seldom had one ever been found guilty of a crime or of doing any harm. The peace and patience with which they died, even when subjected to the cruelest tortures, caused even some of their persecutors to join themselves to the faith.

With intermissions, the persecution continued until the year 311, and in the most eastern districts, under Maximin, until 313. Its effect was to ultimately prove that Christianity was unconquerable.

Throughout much of the world today, Christians are under the continual threat of official, government endorsed or led persecution. The nations where Christianity grew the fastest by percentage over the last ten years were the nations where the persecution was the greatest. Christianity is presently under assault from almost every direction, in almost every country, and yet it still grows at a rate of between two hundred thousand and four hundred thousand people a day! Christianity is now growing three times faster than any other religion in the world, and even faster than the general population is growing in some regions of the world. It can be said of Christianity as it was said of Israel, "The more they afflicted them, the more they increased."

**And not only this, but we also exult in our tribulations, knowing that tribulation brings about perseverance;**

**and perseverance, proven character; and proven character, hope;**

**and hope does not disappoint, because the love of God has been poured out within our hearts through the Holy Spirit who was given to us (Romans 5:3-5).**

**But remember the former days, when, after being enlightened, you endured a great conflict of sufferings,**

**partly, by being made a public spectacle through reproaches and tribulations, and partly by becoming sharers with those who were so treated.**

**For you showed sympathy to the prisoners, and accepted joyfully the seizure of your property, knowing that you have for yourselves a better possession and an abiding one.**

Therefore, do not throw away your confidence, which has a great reward.

For you have need of endurance, so that when you have done the will of God, you may receive what was promised.

For yet in a very little while, He who is coming will come, and will not delay.

But My righteous one shall live by faith; and if he shrinks back, My soul has no pleasure in him.

But we are not of those who shrink back to destruction, but of those who have faith to the preserving of the soul (Hebrews 10:32-39).

## SUMMARY

As we are told in I John 5:19, "**We know that we are of God, and the whole world lies in the power of the evil one.**" We are living in enemy territory. We have been dropped behind enemy lines. We cannot live godly in this world without persecution. It should not be our goal to live without it because persecution is one of the primary ways that the Lord uses the present evil of this world to help conform His people to His image.

If we are going to be like Jesus, we must learn to face persecution, injustice, denial, and betrayal without reacting in the wrong spirit, but rather in the fruit of the Spirit. The Lord could have bound Satan and cast him out immediately after His resurrection. He did not do this for our sakes. This present age is for one purpose, to call and perfect those who will be joint heirs with Jesus. It is training for reigning. We must learn to view every trial as an opportunity to grow in grace.

The Scriptures are clear that at the end of the age the world will be experiencing the deepest darkness and the greatest glory of the Lord at the same time (see Isaiah 60:1-3). It is the darkness that helps to make the light manifest. Just as we see throughout history that persecutions only served to increase and strengthen the church, it will always do this. Let us enjoy peace when we have it, but accept conflict when it comes as the great opportunity that it is. No great leaders were ever revealed until great leadership was required. No great Christians were ever revealed until they were confronted with great darkness. Great darkness is coming, but also glory.

One of the most important things that we can do in preparation for persecution is to develop a sincere love for the truth. We must sink our roots into the Word of God, know what we believe in, and determine that even at the cost of our lives we will not compromise that with which we have been entrusted. As the temptations come to us day by day to compromise just a little, let us hold fast to our confession, always looking to Him. Let us also resolve to hold fast while growing in love and patience for our persecutors, seizing every opportunity to grow in His ways as well as His truth. When the church does this, the world will be assured of seeing His great light through us.

**Take care, brethren, lest there should be in any one of you an evil, unbelieving heart, in falling away from the living God.**

**But encourage one another day after day, as long as it is still called "Today," lest any one of you be hardened by the deceitfulness of sin.**

**For we have become partakers of Christ, if we hold fast the beginning of our assurance firm until the end; (Hebrews 3:12-14)**

Therefore, since we have so great a cloud of witnesses surrounding us, let us also lay aside every encumbrance, and the sin which so easily entangles us, and let us run with endurance the race that is set before us,

fixing our eyes on Jesus, the author and perfecter of faith, who for the joy set before Him endured the cross, despising the shame, and has sat down at the right hand of the throne of God.

For consider Him who has endured such hostility by sinners against Himself, so that you may not grow weary and lose heart.

You have not yet resisted to the point of shedding blood in your striving against sin;

and you have forgotten the exhortation which is addressed to you as sons, "My son, do not regard lightly the discipline of the Lord, nor faint when you are reproved by Him;

For those whom the Lord loves He disciplines, and He scourges every son whom He receives."

It is for discipline that you endure; God deals with you as with sons; for what son is there whom his father does not discipline?

But if you are without discipline, of which all have become partakers, then you are illegitimate children and not sons.

Furthermore, we had earthly fathers to discipline us, and we respected them; shall we not much rather be subject to the Father of spirits, and live?

For they disciplined us for a short time as seemed best to them, but He disciplines us for our good, that we may share His holiness.

All discipline for the moment seems not to be joyful, but sorrowful; yet to those who have been trained by it, afterwards it yields the peaceful fruit of righteousness.

Therefore, strengthen the hands that are weak and the knees that are feeble,

and make straight paths for your feet, so that the limb which is lame may not be put out of joint, but rather be healed.

Pursue peace with all men, and the sanctification without which no one will see the Lord.

See to it that no one comes short of the grace of God; that no root of bitterness springing up causes trouble, and by it many be defiled;

that there be no immoral or godless person like Esau, who sold his own birthright for a single meal.

For you know that even afterwards, when he desired to inherit the blessing, he was rejected, for he found no place for repentance, though he sought for it with tears.

For you have not come to a mountain that may be touched and to a blazing fire, and to darkness and gloom and whirlwind,

and to the blast of a trumpet and the sound of words which sound was such that those who heard begged that no further word should be spoken to them.

For they could not bear the command, "If even a beast touches the mountain, it will be stoned."

And so terrible was the sight, that Moses said, "I am full of fear and trembling."

But you have come to Mount Zion and to the city of the living God, the heavenly Jerusalem, and to myriads of angels,

to the general assembly and church of the first-born who are enrolled in heaven, and to God, the Judge of all, and to the spirits of righteous men made perfect,

and to Jesus, the mediator of a new covenant, and to the sprinkled blood, which speaks better than the blood of Abel (Hebrews 12:1-24).

# CHAPTER TEN

# BEYOND THE BOOK
# OF ACTS

THOSE WHO HAVE TRUE FAITH DO NOT JUST believe that the events written in the Bible are true—they believe that these same works of God can be done through their own lives. This faith has been growing in a great company of witnesses who are soon to be released throughout the earth.

When God was asked His name, He did not reply that His name was "I was" or "I will be," but **"I AM" (Exodus 3:14).** This was a statement for all time that to truly know God we must know Him in the present. It is essential to believe that the events written in the Bible are true and to grasp the great lessons they teach us about God and man's relationship to Him. However, even the comprehension of these great truths is not the goal of faith, but just a foundation. The goal of faith is to know Him and experience Him in our own lives.

Hebrews 11:6 states, **"And without faith it is impossible to please Him, for he who comes to God must believe that He is, and that He is a rewarder of those who seek**

Him." Note here that it says that those who come to God must believe that **"He *is*,"** not that He *was*. As we are told in Hebrews 13:8, **"Jesus Christ is the same yesterday and today, yes and forever."** We therefore do not read the book of Acts to just know what God did in the early church, but as the blueprint for normal church life. Even so, there is also a calling in Scripture to go beyond the book of Acts. This is the Lord's expressed desire, which He stated in John 14:12:

> **"Truly, truly, I say to you, he who believes in Me, the works that I do shall he do also; and greater works than these shall he do; because I go to the Father."**

As great as the acts of the apostles were, none of their works came even close to measuring up to what the Lord Jesus Himself did while on the earth. In fact, one can scour history and not find anyone who did greater works than Jesus. However, we can be sure that this statement of the Son of God will come true. Again, this is obviously not talking about teaching greater truths. The **"greater works"** are works.

Certainly this does not imply that anyone will be greater in faith and works than the Lord, because it will in fact be the Lord working through them when they do the **"greater works."** Neither should we conclude that those who do the **"greater works"** reserved for the end are greater than those who gave birth to the church in the first century. Just as the restored temple was promised to have a greater glory than the former temple, but was itself actually an inferior temple, we are wrong to think that we are superior if we experience something greater. This has more to do with the Lord's timing than the quality of the building materials He has now or had then.

The Lord Himself could have done greater works if it had been the Father's will. When the Jews asked Him for a sign from heaven, they were asking Him to do something like stopping the sun as Joshua did. Jesus could have certainly done this or even greater works but it was not the Father's will. His main purpose for His first coming was to accomplish the atonement and to begin calling those who would be joint heirs with Him. It is because He ascended to the Father that the greater works were made possible for us. The cross fully purchased the right and authority for the redeemed to go forth in power to redeem all that was lost by the Fall, which is the earth and all it contains.

There is a process through which all is being recovered, but the Lord did not want us to be limited in our works to the ones He did. The greatest of all works and miracles have been reserved for the end. One reason for this is because some of the things we are going to be facing at the end are going to require these **"greater works."** Where sin abounds, grace abounds much more. Even so, the Lord has saved His best wine for last. We may not fully know all of the reasons why until we are in the age to come, but it is time for them to be done.

## THE ALPHA AND THE OMEGA

The Lord called Himself **"the Alpha and the Omega,"** **(Revelation 1:8),** which are the first and last letters of the Greek alphabet. One reason for this is probably because there is a special way He manifests Himself at the beginning and the end. We can look at His own life and see that the greatest revelations of His purpose came at His birth and then at the cross. This is why we also have a "former rain" and a **"latter rain"** in Scripture (see Joel 2:23). These all speak of the way He would move in great ways, at the beginning of the age and then at the end.

This does not mean the Lord did not manifest Himself during all of the centuries in-between, just as His whole life while He walked on the earth was full of meaning and remarkable deeds. Even so, there are special manifestations at the beginning and the end, and we are coming to the end of this age.

The book of Acts is the glorious story of the beginning of the church. It is an incomparably wonderful and inspiring heritage. The first century church set a standard that has not yet been duplicated. A high goal to reach for is to see the things that were done in the early church be accomplished in our own lives and times. This is about much more than just seeing miracles. It is about the level of devotion, wisdom, knowledge, sacrifice, labors, and the courage with which they stood up to even the rulers of empires when persecuted. The best of all was the way the Lord manifested Himself among His people.

Any church that attained to what the first century church accomplished would without question be the greatest church in the earth today. However, every church today is called to emulate what the early church had and to go beyond. There is going to be a last day book of Acts experience for the church greater than what was experienced in the first century.

We do need to acknowledge that at least presently, overall, we still have a long way to go to be able to walk in what they did in the first century, but this is going to dramatically change. We must raise our expectations for church life in our own time and our own congregations now.

We are approaching the times when the greatest works of God that ever will be done on the earth through men are released. Those who are going to be a part of this are going to be the ones who with undying resolve and determination keep pressing toward the mark of the high calling of God in Christ Jesus.

## THE NEXT STEP

To get to the place we are called to be spiritually, we need a map. For a map to be useful, we must first find our destination on it. Then we must locate where we are presently and decide the best way to get to the destination. Bible prophecy and church history are our maps. I include church history because if we do not know what has already been fulfilled, we cannot know where we are and what the next step is to be. The two books that I published with Thomas Nelson, *A Prophetic Vision for the Twenty-first Century,* and *Shadows of Things to Come,* were both written to help the church see and begin to use this map.

As the saying goes, "Those who do not know history are doomed to repeat it." This is certainly true of the church. The progress of the church falters, and the great movements that have arisen have all been stopped because we continue to fall to the same mistakes. This alone is reason enough for us to seek a knowledge of church history, but this is not even the most important reason for doing so. We cannot truly understand the map of Bible prophecy without it.

One of the reasons I have studied history extensively for thirty years is because the Lord told me that I could not understand prophecy without this knowledge. I was shown how the roots of a tree below the ground are just as extensive as the branches above it. I was told if I wanted to grow strong and be able to endure the storms that were coming, I had to dig deep. I could only be trusted with revelation of things to come to the degree that I had sunk my roots into both the Scriptures and a knowledge of history.

Do you then need to spend thirty years studying history? No. In fact, you may only need a few hours here and there. One of the ways the Lord has saved His best wine for last are through books. For example, take the recent New York Times bestseller, **Constantine's Sword,** by James Carroll. This is a classic work which unquestionably took the author many years to research and put together. However, you can absorb all of the knowledge it took him so long to accumulate in just a few hours by reading his book.

The Lord is giving His people increasing revelation and interpretation concerning Bible prophecy and its relation to church history. Where we are headed does need more clarity than to just say we are going to have another book of Acts experience. For us to go forward, we must have a clear understanding of where we are. Only then will our future direction be clear.

## WHERE ARE WE?

We are told in II Corinthians 13:5: **"Test yourselves to see if you are in the faith; examine yourselves!"** There is a time for projecting vision, and there is a time for examination of ourselves and our works. We need to be able to do both together. We need to see where we are going and have a good evaluation of where we are.

In recent years there have been a number of great moves of God that have been quite different from each other. Even so, they have all worked together to prepare us for what is to come. There will be many more breaking out in various places. Those who are going to be the most prepared to be a part of what is coming are those who had the wisdom and humility to visit and receive from these movements. For those who are gaining vision and perspective from the Holy Spirit, these different moves of God will start to make both a pattern and a trail which becomes increasingly clear.

In speaking of these movements, I am not only referring to those such as Brownsville and Toronto, though these are certainly important, there are also others in Asia, South and Central America, Africa, Eastern Europe, and the South Pacific. Seeds have been sown and the groundwork laid for a significant move of God to come out of Scandinavia that will be crucial for Europe. Russia and Turkey are going to experience some of the greatest moves of God in the last days, as will the entire region biblically called "Assyria," which we know from biblical prophecies such as Isaiah 11 and 19 that have not yet come to pass.

The greatest fires of revival are going to break out and be sustained in the places where many different "coals from the fires" have been brought together from the different, previous moves of God. To be in the mainstream of what the Lord is doing in the earth, we must excel more and more at crossing national and denominational barriers for the interchange and "cross-pollination" of the Spirit. Those who continue in isolation will drift further and further from the River of Life the Lord is now bringing forth in the earth.

Studying church history is one way we honor our spiritual fathers and mothers and submit to the body of Christ that has been forming since the day of Pentecost. Visiting with humility and a teachable spirit the moves of God that are arising presently is a way we submit to the body of Christ in our own times. The humility, to which God gives His grace, will be found among the teachable. This is also how we must become like little children to enter the kingdom. To become like a child in this way is not to be immature, or foolish, but to be as inquisitive and teachable as a child.

If Jesus, John the Baptist, or Paul the apostle lived in our times and we heard that they were coming to a city a thousand miles away, we would be the most spiritually foolish not to go see them. The Lord said that those who received even the least of His people were receiving Him. The apostle Paul commended the Galatians for receiving him as if he were an angel from heaven. My point is that a "move of God" really is God moving, and those who have the hunger and humility to go where God is moving will be the ones who find the grace to walk in what is coming.

## THE SPIRITUAL DELTA FORCE

For the last few years I have been given visions of a very unique and still quite small spiritual force that is being prepared in different places around the world. Those who are a part of this force have the most fierce resolution in their purpose than any I have ever witnessed. In fact, whenever I think of them, this is the first thing that comes to mind—they are profoundly sure of who they are and where they are going.

They also have an uncompromising devotion to truth and integrity. Even though they tend to be severe in their demeanor, they are driven by their love for God and His people. You certainly do not feel "sloppy agape" when around them. Their love is so great that they will without hesitation risk their lives for a single one of the Lord's sheep. They are supremely confident because of their training and yet they are so humble they truly esteem others as more important.

They may also be the most supernaturally powerful people who have ever walked on the earth at one time. These will be known as "the messengers of His power." These will be walking "coals of fire" from the very throne of God who help to set off revival and moves of God wherever they are sent.

These messengers of power are presently alive and are scattered all over the earth. It is hard to find more than a handful who are together in any one place at this time, though they will begin to congregate more in a few places. Even so, a congregation that has just two of these at this time is exceptional. Many congregations cannot stand the fire that is on these emerging ones and either have or will try to drive them away. Most are presently living the Luke 7:31-35 experience:

> **To what then shall I compare the men of this generation, and what are they like?**
>
> **They are like children who sit in the market place and call to one another; and they say, 'We played the flute for you, and you did not dance; we sang a dirge, and you did not weep.'**
>
> **For John the Baptist has come eating no bread and drinking no wine; and you say, 'He has a demon!'**
>
> **The Son of Man has come eating and drinking; and you say, Behold, a gluttonous man, and a drunkard, a friend of tax-gatherers and sinners!'**
>
> **Yet wisdom is vindicated by all her children.**

In this same way they are having a hard time fitting in with the church in its present state. They are marching to a different drumbeat, a different sound. The enemy will try to take advantage of this to make them bitter and rebellious, as he knows this will be the most effective way that they can be disqualified from their purpose. Even though they resist becoming bitter or rebellious, most are far too focused and serious to fit into the typical local church life as it is at this time. Because of this, the Lord is even now preparing places for them where they can join with others who are called as they are. These are God's "special forces." If we understand them, many unnecessary problems can be avoided and the whole church can greatly benefit from their ministry.

One of the most important tasks of our military special forces is to train other native forces in special operations and tactics. Likewise, these spiritual special forces will be sent all over the world to train native Christian leaders where great spiritual advances are about to begin. They are the true apostles, prophets, evangelists, pastors, and teachers who will fulfill the Ephesians Four mandate to equip the saints to do the work of the ministry. They are being sent to equip those who will lead the last day ministry. Their great effectiveness in equipping the saints to fulfill their calling will itself be a power that starts to radically transform the church.

## WISDOM IS VINDICATED BY HER CHILDREN

The oldest of those whom I was shown in this great company are still in their twenties. Most are still children and many are still being born. This leads me to believe that their purpose will unfold more and more over the next few decades. It is true that we are coming to the close of this age, but it is also critical that we understand we still have a few decades. We must therefore prepare for the future with strategy and vision, not an escape mentality.

There are "Joshuas" and "Calebs" from the previous generation that are helping to prepare these messengers of power for their calling. When Israel failed to enter the Promised Land the first time, Joshua and Caleb did not start complaining about their own generation, they started to work immediately to help prepare the next one that would enter the land. Likewise, many of those who are a part of the present generation are called to help prepare the coming generation and will then lead them through what is coming.

Some of those who are called to lead the greatest generation are already quite elderly. They are going to be renewed, and there will be a powerful anointing on them to help renew the church. That the bride of Christ is without "spot" speaks of her purity. That she is without "wrinkle" speaks of her perpetual youthfulness (see Ephesians 5:27). This youthful anointing is coming upon the church in a very supernatural way. The elderly are going to start growing younger, and even their physical bodies are going to be quickened by the One who is able to quicken our mortal bodies. One touch from the Lord can renew us like no Oil of Olay ever could. No one who is alive is too old for what is coming. We can be renewed in our strength.

Even so, most of those whom I have been shown in this great company are very young physically. Even these young ones had a fierce resolution in their demeanor. One characteristic they all shared, and by which they recognized one another, was their serious, unyielding focus upon their purpose. This is impossible to duplicate unless you are profoundly sure of who you are, what you are doing, and why.

Even though there will be "Joshuas and Calebs" from the present generation, just as Joshua and Caleb were literally "one in a million" from their generation, there will not be many of these. Even so, some of the Christian leaders who are presently leading the church are among the greatest who have ever lived. Like John the Baptist, they are all here to prepare the way for what is coming, and like John the Baptist, they will prophesy over the coming ones, but still not really understand them or their message. Even so, many in the present generation of leaders are doing their job and doing it well.

Again, it is imperative for those who will fulfill their purpose and destiny from the present generation in leadership to understand their purpose to prepare and equip the next generation. Youth and children's ministry will become the heart and soul of every congregation who will be a part of what will become the greatest move of God to ever come upon the world.

One recurring vision I have had is of an eight to ten year old girl fighting demons with the courage, endurance, and wisdom of the most seasoned warrior. This little girl never had a chance to play with dolls and did not want to. She was liberating souls and giving courage to a great company who lived every day for one purpose—to do all things for the sake of the gospel. I have seen little boys who never played army because they were in one. They were fighters. They were wise far beyond their years. The seriousness in the faces of these children was unnerving. Even so, the peace and the joy that was on them was beyond anything that children at play can ever experience. These children truly are for signs and wonders.

## THE NAMELESS, FACELESS ONES

I have heard Paul Cain share many times about the recurring vision he has had of "the nameless, faceless ones."

These fill stadiums with people to hear the gospel. They heal all manners of disease and even raise the dead, but the people do not even know their names. This is a true vision. I believe that I was shown this same group before I met Paul or had heard of his vision and wrote about them in my book, *The Harvest.* Recently, I have had repeated visions of these coming ones, each vision giving me a little more insight into who they are. I have used the term "spiritual Delta Force" here because I was also shown that there are a number of parallels between these coming "messengers of power" and the United States Army's Delta Force.

The United States still does not officially acknowledge that the Delta Force even exists, though everyone now knows it does. Likewise, the church in general will seldom even acknowledge that its "spiritual Delta Force" exists. The Delta Force is the elite of the elite among our military forces and are among the best fighters and secret operators in the world. They do not ever want to be acknowledged or given recognition for their exploits. Why? Because as soon as they become known they can no longer do their job. The Lord is likewise raising up an elite force of the best of the best from the last day church. Like the Delta Force, they fear becoming known because it will compromise their ability to do their job. They live for but one purpose—to do what they were put on this earth to do. They actually fear recognition.

## OUR GREATEST ENEMY–JEALOUSY

The very word "elite" is offensive to many Christians, but the calling, training, and equipping of this elite force of Christians is in fact one of the most important things that is going on in the earth today. It is understandable why many would want to shy away from this word with all of the examples we have of prideful groups who think they are the elite. Nevertheless, the Lord Himself picked a few "chosen ones" from out of the many who were called, and spent a great deal of His time preparing them for their purpose. For us to be prepared for our purpose in these times, we must start doing things the way the Lord did, especially in the way we prepare and release leadership.

The story of the birth, development, and deployment of the Delta Force is one of the great stories of endurance and focused, prophetic vision by a small group of individuals in United States military history. It is also a prophetic parallel of what is going to be emerging in the body of Christ.

The founders of this unique, small, but powerful force, prophetically foresaw the war against terrorism decades before we entered this present conflict. They tried to get their country ready for it, but for years very few would listen to them. Against continual opposition from their fellow officers, and even the civilian leaders of the United States military, they held their course and ultimately prevailed. When the time came they were ready and are now the front-line force in this war. Most do not even know anything about what they are doing. That is the way they want it. They are not doing it for publicity or accolades—they are trying to save their country.

The main reason that the development of the Delta Force received so much continual opposition from the rest of the Army can be summed up in one word—jealousy. Already there were some elite units such as the Airborne, the Rangers, and of course, the Green Berets, who all claimed nothing else was needed because they could do the job. They became even more offended when the best of their troops were being recruited for a secret force that was even more focused and elite than they were.

The greatest battle for survival by the Delta Force came against the United States Army itself. It took one of the greatest examples of visionary leadership in our history on the part of one colonel, and a few other generals who also had prophetic vision, for the Delta Force to survive, much less become the extraordinary force it is today. The same will be required of those who are called to lead the spiritual special forces that are now being raised up for what is to come. The greatest battle for survival will come from jealousy within the church.

This is nothing new. We are told in Scripture that even the Lord was crucified because of envy (see Matthew 27:18, Mark 15:10). Even so, we need to recognize the incredible destruction that jealousy continues to bring within the church. It is possibly the single greatest sign of a lack of true authority and one of the most powerful, evil strongholds in the church that we can be sure will resist the true apostolic.

Those who are offended by the word "elite" will become some of the greatest obstacles to the preparation of the last day ministry. However, dealing with this is part of the training. There is an elite force of Christians being raised up who are, and must be, very different from the typical, lukewarm, Christians on the earth today. They will not only have higher standards, they will have *much* higher standards. When these are released, one of them really will put a thousand to flight, and two of them will chase ten thousand.

Many will let jealousy drive them to become opposers of what is to come, but many others will be pricked in their hearts by the focused devotion of these messengers of power and will wake up from their sleep and lukewarm attitudes. The ultimate result is going to be the whole church being transformed from what appears spiritually to be a confused mob to being the disciplined and powerful force that it is called to be.

## KNOW YOUR PLACE

Just as the Delta Force could not by itself win a war against any other major power, but would need the entire United States military, the church cannot win its last day spiritual battles with just its "elite" forces. The tactics in which the Delta Force are trained would be useless on the typical battlefield. Likewise, the gifts and spiritual expertise of the coming "messengers of power" simply will not work in the church in general and in many of the spiritual battles that will need to be fought. Even though most of the church today is asleep to the times, and needs to be awakened by this great force being raised up, very few Christians are called to be a part of it.

Does this mean that most Christians are called to be inferior spiritual warriors? Not at all—just different. Many of the greatest spiritual exploits will be done by those slugging it out day by day on the front lines of their local churches. Those who display the courage to hold the lines against great onslaughts, and are then willing to leave the safety of the trenches to attack the strongholds of the enemy, are no less heroes than those who are involved in special operations. Many of the great heroes in military history were cooks or other support personnel who picked up weapons and fought like lions when they were needed. Some of the great leaders and heroes of the faith in the last days will likewise arise from unexpected sources.

Even so, the church needs to understand that there is an "elite force" being prepared and we need to know how to relate to them. I am sorry there does not seem to be a better word to use than this, but I will never apologize for the fact that such a spiritual force is going to be raised up. They will not accomplish the entire victory, but they are going to do much to make the way for it. Few will even know what they did or that they were ever there which is fine with them.

Let us also keep in mind that generals who lead large forces, or command a ship, fly the sophisticated aircraft, etc., are certainly just as important as those who lead small, special units. We all need each other, and we all need to be secure within our own place.

Even so, just as the special forces of the United States military have injected something of a devotion to excellence that helped to raise the standards of the entire military, the special spiritual forces now being raised up will help awaken and raise the standards of all true believers.

## RANK IN THE KINGDOM?

Democracy is one of the great gifts of God to mankind. With fallen mankind it is the best and safest form of government. The freedoms that have come through the release of democracy in the earth is also helping to prepare the world for the coming of the kingdom because **"where the Spirit of the Lord is, there is liberty" (II Corinthians 3:17).** Even so, the kingdom is not a democracy and it never will be.

The Scriptures are clear—there is an aristocracy in heaven, and many of the rewards for our faithfulness on earth will last for eternity. The most basic of those rewards is our position in heaven. We will not all be the same there, and the Scriptures are very clear about it. There are positions in heaven even as to who sits at the right hand and the left (which are being determined by our life on earth).

This rank and position in heaven is what the apostle Paul was talking about when he said in Philippians 3:13-14, **"Brethren, I do not regard myself as having laid hold of it yet; but one thing I do: forgetting what lies behind and reaching forward to what lies ahead, I press on toward the goal for the prize of the upward call of God in Christ Jesus."** Paul was not talking about salvation here, as he was fully redeemed and saved the moment he first believed in the atonement of the cross. What he calls **"the upward call,"** or "the high calling," was in fact just that. Paul understood that there was much more to pursue than just salvation, and this was the driving force behind his great devotion.

Anyone who begins to perceive this high calling will be compelled to lay aside every encumbrance to run the race for the prize. There is no greater endeavor in the universe that can compare to the opportunity that we have been given to attain in Christ. For those who perceive the call, there will be no greater ambition than to hear on that great judgment day, **"Well done good and faithful servant..."** **(Matthew 25:21 NIV).** In fact, anyone who has perceived the exalted King Whom we serve, and is not burning with the consuming passion to do all things for His sake, has certainly fallen to a terrible delusion. Those who truly follow the King live to do their Master's will.

Even so, to win this race we have been called to run, we must rise above the pursuit of our own rank and position. This seems like a paradox and it is. To win this race we must become so empty of selfish ambition and so full of love for God and our fellow soldiers of the cross, that we do all things for His glory and their benefit, not just for a position that we gain. To win the race, we will have to grow in love for our fellow men, and we would willingly give our own place to them. It is by seeking our own lives that we lose, and by being willing to lose our lives for His sake that we gain. The highest rank really is for the purpose of being the servant of all.

It is an interesting characteristic of the United States Army Delta Force that they do not observe typical military protocols. They do not salute officers, and even the lowest ranking enlisted man calls a colonel by his first name. How can such an elite force be so lacking in these basic military disciplines? When you are the best, you really cease to care about titles and rank. Likewise, those who attain to the highest positions in the kingdom have done so partly by ceasing to care about such things. This is probably why even the great apostle Paul, near the end of his life, did not consider himself to have attained to the high calling, but was determined to press on (see Philippians 3:13-14).

Of course, one reason that the Delta Force does not observe military protocols is because they do not want to be perceived as even being military, and they do not want someone to slip-up by calling someone "Sir," giving away their true identity. Even so, if a sergeant in the Delta Force has the most expertise in a certain area that a mission requires, then he will lead that mission and the colonel will follow him. In a sense they have risen above rank to the place where they recognize that the anointing leads. This is because they have risen to the place where the main thing is to keep the main thing the main thing—which is to get the job done.

Likewise, those who are the greatest apostles, prophets, etc., who are about to be released on the earth care little for such titles. In fact, they would much rather not be known by them. They do not do things to try to get recognized, but will purposely seek to become of "no reputation." Yet, they will be used to do the most extraordinary miracles, at times filling stadiums and leading multitudes to salvation, but leave before anyone finds out who they are. It is enough for them to be known by their King and to simply be able to do His will. They want their reward in heaven, not on the earth.

## The Army Needs Protocol

If the regular army tried to operate like the Delta Force, it would quickly degenerate into a useless mob that would be easy prey for any much smaller force that had military discipline. Even though the titles such as apostle, prophet, and bishop have become so overused and cheap in our time, we still need them. There are positions of authority in the church that must be recognized if we are going to receive the benefit of them.

We are told in Matthew 10:41, **"He who receives a prophet in the name of a prophet shall receive a prophet's reward; and he who receives a righteous man in the name of a righteous man shall receive a righteous man's reward."** The same is true for every ministry. We must receive an apostle in the name of an apostle to receive an apostle's reward. If we receive an apostle as just a teacher, then all we will get is teaching and miss what we could have received.

For this reason it is not wrong to recognize people in their positions of authority in the church. However, the more true spiritual authority that a person has, the less they will care about human recognition. Those who are the most demanding of recognition will inevitably have the least and may even be false. Jezebel **"calls herself a prophetess" (Revelation 2:20).** We must learn to examine those who call themselves apostles and are not, as well as those who call themselves prophets or by any other title.

## SUMMARY

I have often been accused of trying to raise up "elite Christians." I want to make it very clear that I am guilty as charged. The more I have been shown about this spiritual force which is about to arise, the more devoted to it I have become. However, I do not see myself as being their leader or even being a leader among them. I am simply trying to help make a place for them because I have been shown their importance.

Colonel Beckwith is considered the founder of the United States Army Delta Force. However, he could never have done it without the few generals in the army who were not Special Forces officers. They prophetically understood the importance of this special unit and did all that they could to aid its development. I view myself more like one of these officers who has prophetically foreseen our need for this force and will do all I can to aid in its development. I do hope that MorningStar is one of the places where those who are so called can gather and develop. We are making a special place for them.

Our MorningStar School of Ministry is developing a radical missions program to help train such a spiritual force. We are making a special place for them because it was made clear to us that this is part of our calling. However, we have seen that the benefit they are to us and our ministry is much greater than anything we will be able to do for them.

Can you apply for this program? No. You cannot choose to come; we have to choose you. It is not for everyone, and we only want to include those who we feel are called to it. It is easy to discern those who are so called because they are different. While others are growing spiritually, these are growing radically. While others are having a good time, these are studying, praying, going out onto the streets and witnessing, casting out demons, and praying for the sick to be healed. That is their good time.

There are some aspects of our ministry, such as our Christian day school, the Comenius School for Creative Leadership, that I have been commanded to steer more and more toward the development of the children who are called to be a part of this force. There are many other great Christian schools around to which most of our kids need to go. I have even had to steer some of my own children to other schools because they were not called to be in this school. This was a hard thing for me. It is hard for many of our other parents and even our teachers to understand. I honestly do not expect many to understand, at least not until some future events begin to unfold.

I am not steering our entire ministry to fit this group, but there are some necessary things that we have had to do to accommodate them. These things are certainly not to everyone's liking, but they will be to everyone's benefit. Misunderstanding is a price everyone will likely have to pay to be a part of helping to raise up the last day ministry of the church.

The perfect church is perfectly modeled after the Lord's own ministry. He had a ministry to the multitudes, and He had another, smaller group to which He gave more attention. He then had a very small group that He shared everything with. This is why I believe that the Tabernacle of Moses and the temples that were built all had three sections.

If we only want to minister to the "elite" and do not have something for the multitudes, we will become imbalanced and possibly delusional and divisive. If we only minister to the multitudes and do not have a group that we are helping go further, deeper, and higher, then we will tend to be very shallow, and possibly even promote a lukewarmness and an unsanctified mercy.

Just as the Outer Court was the largest section of the Tabernacle, and where the most people will be found, I think the largest part of every ministry needs to be that which will draw in the multitudes. However, once someone is in, they need to understand that they can go as far in the Lord as they desire to go. It is a calling.

Those who would go on also need to know that the standards for those who will minister in the Holy of Holies are very different. The things you can get away with in the Outer Court can get you killed in the Holy Place. The way is open to all, but you must go to the Altar and die, you must go to the Laver and be cleansed, and you must understand that when you enter the Holy Place there will be no natural light there. The only light that can be seen when we have entered is the light of the anointing of the Holy Spirit. As we proceed on into the final, smallest, compartment, the only light is that of the glory of the Lord.

Just to be able to stand and minister in the anointing and in the glory is beyond what many can do. Many do collapse and are "slain in the Spirit" just by getting close. However, we must learn to stand and do our duties even in His manifest presence. The mature have learned not to fall down. More than anything else we need those who can stand—stand in His presence, as well as stand against any onslaught of the devil. The Lord is again asking the great question that He asked through Jeremiah:

**"But who has stood in the council of the Lord, that he should see and hear His word? Who has given heed to His word and listened?**

**"Behold, the storm of the Lord has gone forth in wrath, even a whirling tempest; It will swirl down on the head of the wicked.**

**"The anger of the LORD will not turn back until He has performed and carried out the purposes of His heart; in the last days you will clearly understand it.**

**"I did not send these prophets, but they ran. I did not speak to them, but they prophesied.**

**"But if they had stood in My council, then they would have announced My words to My people, and would have turned them back from their evil way, and from the evil of their deeds (Jeremiah 23:18-22).**